First Print Edition [1.0] -1441h. (2019c.e.)

Copyright © 1441 H./2019 C.E.
Taalib al-Ilm Educational Resources

**http://taalib.com
Learn Islaam, Live Islaam.**^{SM}

All rights reserved, this publication may be not reproduced, stored in a retrieval system, or transmitted in any form or by any means, electronic, mechanical, photocopying, recording, scanning, or otherwise, except with the prior written permission of the Publisher.

Requests to the Publisher for permission should be addressed to the Permissions Department, Taalib al-Ilm Educational Resources by e-mail: **service@taalib.com**.

Taalib al-Ilm Education Resources products are made available through distributors worldwide. To view a list of current distributors in your region, or information about our distributor/referral program please visit our website. Discounts on bulk quantities of our products are available to community groups, religious institutions, and other not-for-profit entities, inshAllaah. For details and discount information, contact the special sales department by e-mail: **service@taalib.com**.

The publisher requests that any corrections regarding translations or knowledge based issues, be sent to us at: **service@taalib.com**. Readers should note that internet web sites offered as citations and/or sources for further information may have changed or no longer be available between the time this was written and when it is read. We publish a variety of full text and free preview edition electronic ebook formats. Some content that appears in print may not be available in electronic book versions.

ISBN EAN-13:   978-1-938117-90-9   [Soft cover Print Edition]

From the Publisher

GOLDEN WORDS UPON GOLDEN WORDS...FOR EVERY MUSLIM.

"Imaam al-Barbahaaree, may Allaah have mercy upon him said:

May Allaah have mercy upon you! Examine carefully the speech of everyone you hear from in your time particularly. So do not act in haste and do not enter into anything from it until you ask and see: Did any of the Companions of the Prophet, may Allaah's praise and salutations be upon him, speak about it, or did any of the scholars? So if you find a narration from them about it, cling to it, do not go beyond it for anything and do not give precedence to anything over it and thus fall into the Fire.

Explanation by Sheikh Saaleh al-Fauzaan, may Allaah preserve him:

'Do not be hasty in accepting as correct what you may hear from the people especially in these later times. As now there are many who speak about so many various matters, issuing rulings and ascribing to themselves both knowledge and the right to speak. This is especially the case after the emergence and spread of new modern day media technologies.

Such that everyone now can speak and bring forth that which is in truth worthless; by this meaning words of no true value - speaking about whatever they wish in the name of knowledge and in the name of the religion of Islaam. It has even reached the point that you find the people of misguidance and the members of the various groups of misguidance and deviance from the religion speaking as well. Such individuals have now become those who speak in the name of the religion of Islaam through means such as the various satellite television channels. Therefore be very cautious!

It is upon you oh Muslim, and upon you oh student of knowledge individually, to verify matters and not rush to embrace everything and anything you may hear. It is upon you to verify the truth of what you hear, asking, 'Who else also makes this same statement or claim?', 'Where did this thought or concept originate or come from?', 'Who is its reference or source authority?'. Asking what are the evidences which support it from within the Book and the Sunnah? And inquiring where has the individual who is putting this forth studied and taken his knowledge from? From who has he studied the knowledge of Islaam?

Each of these matters requires verification through inquiry and investigation, especially in the present age and time. As it is not every speaker who should rightly be considered a source of knowledge, even if he is well spoken and eloquent, and can manipulate words captivating his listeners. Do not be taken in and accept him until you are aware of the degree and scope of what he possesses of knowledge and understanding. As perhaps someone's words may be few, but possess true understanding, and perhaps another will have a great deal of speech yet he is actually ignorant to such a degree that he doesn't actually posses anything of true understanding. Rather he only has the ability to enchant with his speech so that the people are deceived. Yet he puts forth the perception that he is a scholar, that he is someone of true understanding and comprehension, that he is a capable thinker, and so forth. Through such means and ways he is able to deceive and beguile the people, taking them away from the way of truth.

Therefore what is to be given true consideration is not the amount of the speech put forth or that one can extensively discuss a subject. Rather the criterion that is to be given consideration is what that speech contains within it of sound authentic knowledge, what it contains of the established and transmitted principles of Islaam. As perhaps a short or brief statement which is connected to or has a foundation in the established principles can be of greater benefit than a great deal of speech which simply rambles on, and through hearing you don't actually receive very much benefit from.

This is the reality which is present in our time; one sees a tremendous amount of speech which only possesses within it a small amount of actual knowledge. We see the presence of many speakers yet few people of true understanding and comprehension.' "

[The eminent major scholar Sheikh Saaleh al-Fauzaan, may Allaah preserve him- 'A Valued Gift for the Reader Of Comments Upon the Book Sharh as-Sunnah', page 102-103]

This pocket edition is based upon appendixes taken from the larger book:

The Cure, The Explanation, The Clear Affair, & The Brilliantly Distinct Signpost:

Book 2: The Meaning Of Worship & Innovation In Islaam

Based upon
'Usul as-Sunnah' of Imaam Ahmad
(may Allaah have mercy upon him)

The original course book, is part of a full series, intended to be a vital learning tool, by Allaah's persmission, for discussing and learning many of the most important sources of Islaam, how to implement them, and how to avoid common mistakes and misunderstandings.

This full course series is based upon various commentaries of the original text, from the following scholars of our age, may Allaah have mercy upon then or preserve them:

Sheikh Zayd Ibn Muhammad al-Madkhalee
Sheikh Saleeh Ibn Sa'd As-Suhaaymee
Sheikh 'Abdul-'Azeez Ibn 'Abdullah ar-Raajhee
Sheikh Rabee'a Ibn Haadee al-Madkhalee
Sheikh Sa'd Ibn Naasir as-Shathree
Sheikh 'Ubayd Ibn 'Abdullah al-Jaabiree
Sheikh 'Abdullah al-Bukharee
Sheikh Hamd al-'Uthmaan...and other scholars

Each course book lesson has: lesson text, scholastic commentary, evidence summary, lesson benefits, standard & review exercises, as well as the Arabic text & translation of 'Usul as-Sunnah' in Arabic divided for easier memorization.

Compiled and Translated by:
Abu Sukhailah Khalil Ibn-Abelahyi

[Available: **Now**, pages: **470+**
price: (Soft cover) **$27.50**
(Hard cover) **$45**
(Kindle) **$9.99**]

TRUE WORSHIP, BUILD YOUR ISLAAM PROPERLY, CALLING TO THE SUNNAH, & MODERN SCHOLARS

LET THE SCHOLARS SPEAK- CLARITY & GUIDANCE (BOOK 4)

Translated & Compiled By
Abu Sukhailah Khalil Ibn-Abelahyi

Table of Contents

Amended Preface..10

Guidance To Worship Correctly Comes From Allaah Alone.......... 42

Embrace Islaam Completely & Fully Not Partially 54

The Remembrance of Allaah & Merits of Gatherings of Dhikr......66

Do not Build your Islaam Upon Your Intellect or Emotions- But Upon Revelation..82

The Danger of Intentionally Following Ambiguous Meanings........90

Don't Let Your Brother Drown Pull Him Towards the Sunnah.....104

Modern Scholars Who Are Carriers Of The Flag Of Criticism And Commendation In Our Religion..130

AMENDED PREFACE

In the name of Allaah, The Most Gracious, The Most Merciful

Verily, all praise is due to Allaah, we praise Him, we seek His assistance and we ask for His forgiveness. We seek refuge in Him from the evils of our souls and the evils of our actions. Whoever Allaah guides, no one can lead him astray and whoever is caused to go astray, there is no one that can guide him. I bear witness that there is no deity worthy of worship except Allaah alone with no partners. And I bear witness that Muhammad is His worshipper and Messenger.

◈ *Oh you who believe, fear Allaah as He ought to be feared and do not die except while you are Muslims.* ◈ -(Surah Aal-'Imraan:102)

◈ *Oh mankind, fear Allaah who created you from a single soul and from that, He created its mate. And from them He brought forth many men and women. And fear Allaah to whom you demand your mutual rights. Verily, Allaah is an ever All-Watcher over you.* ◈ -(Surah an-Nisaa:1)

◈ *Oh you who believe, fear Allaah and speak a word that is truthful (and to the point) - He will rectify your deeds and forgive you your sins. And whoever obeys Allaah and His Messenger has achieved a great success.* ◈ -(Surah al-Ahzaab:70-71)

As for what follows:

THE SUCCESS OF MUSLIMS IS FOUNDED UPON AUTHENTIC BELIEFS AND ACTIONS UPON THEM

The second course book in the Usul as-Sunnah Series, with the help and support of Allaah, is focused upon examining our understanding of the very nature worship within Islaam, the different types of actions and endeavors in life, the two categories of our worship, and the important question of whether ritual worship changes and evolves or is something set and unchanging within the perfect guidance of our revealed religion of Islaam. Among the beneficial statements from the verifying scholars throughout the centuries upon the Sunnah, about our purpose and blessings, Sheikh 'Abdur-Rahman Ibn Yahya al-Mu'alamee al-Yamaanee, may Allaah have mercy upon him, said,[1]

> *"Certainly Allaah created you in order that you worship Him.*
>
> *And certainly He established the proofs and evidence in a way to be apparent to you, in order that you should direct your worship to Him alone.*
>
> *And certainly He has granted and blessed you with numerous blessings in order that you praise Him."*

The responsibility to learn about and then practice the reality of worship in our lives is in our own individual hands, no matter who we are and where we are. As one of the leading scholars of our age Sheikh Saaleh al-Fauzaan, may Allaah preserve him, said,[2]

> *"It is the individual who brings himself towards ruin, or rescues himself from Allaah's punishment.*
>
> *As it is by working and engaging in whatever is the obedience of Allaah that you save yourself.*

[1] al-Khatib wa al-Wasaayah pg. 190
[2] Tasheel al-Ilmaam: vol. 1 pg 505

Just as it is by engaging in matters which are sins that your soul is pushed towards ruin and destruction.

Each of us can only stand in one of these two situations."

Yet so many of us as Muslims haven't taken the time to question how correct our understanding of our religion is, and ask what is truly worship. Many of us make the critical mistake of simply and unquestioningly following some of those around us in whatever they hold to be true. Imaam ash-Shaa'tibee, may Allaah have mercy upon him, said,[3]

"A person slipping and stumbling in the affairs of the religion is often caused by opposing the evidence in some matter and just relying upon the positions of men among people. Due to this, he is taken off of the clear way of the Companions and their Successors and instead comes to follow his own desires without firm knowledge. Such that by this he strays from the straight correct path!"

The satisfaction with the unsupported opinions of people, along with other misconceptions connected to knowledge, are some of the most dangerous afflictions and problems that Muslims continue to be faced with today. Sheikh al-Albaanee, may Allaah have mercy upon him, said,[4]

"The most dangerous and significant affliction of the Muslim world- and some of them will denounce and reject what I am stating- the most significant affliction of the Muslim world today is more dangerous than the occupation by the Jews of the land of Palestine!

The most significant affliction of the Muslim world today is that they have gone astray from the straight path of Islaam. They do not understand Islaam properly such that they would be able to realize contentment and success in both this world and the next world of the Hereafter...

[3] al-'Istisaam: vol. 2 pg. 864
[4] Transcribed lecture from within the book 'Our Painful Reality': page 34

....as for that Muslim who lives comfortably in this world yet is distant from even understanding Islaam as Allaah, the Most High and the Most Exalted, and His Messenger intended, then when he dies it is an unfortunate wretched death, even if he lived well materially and was outwardly successful."

Our scholars continually clearly present the reality of what is true wellness and well-being in different ways, and in many types of reminders. All the steadfast scholars upon the Sunnah affirm and teach us, that which Ibn al-Qayyim, may Allaah have mercy upon him, stated so eloquently,[5]

"The diseases of the heart are more dangerous than the illnesses or afflictions of the body. This is undoubtedly true. Since the worse case that occurs with a physical illness is that it results in the one afflicted dying.

But as for the illnesses of the heart they may eventually lead to the one afflicted with them being punished for eternity. And there is no cure for the illnesses of the heart other than Sharee'ah knowledge."

Similarly, we find that Sheikh al-'Utheimeen, may Allaah have mercy upon him, likewise said,[6]

"If you see the people rushing and crowding at the doors of hospitals, yet being heedless and turning away from the doors of the masjids, then know that their general situation isn't good nor healthy.

As this indicates that they are diligent and concerned about healing their physical illnesses and problems, without having the same concern and efforts directed towards healing the inner illnesses of their hearts. This is a clear indication of the general deterioration and state of ruin in their lives, and we seek refuge in Allaah from that."

---
[5] Miftah Dar as-Sa'adah: vol 1. pg. 111
[6] Fath Dhil-Jalaal wal-'Ikraam: vol. 3 pg. 273

When we look at the condition of the Muslim Ummah, we often see a lack of understanding and focus upon cultivating both inner and outer worship. It is then, we recognize the importance and value of the consistent clarity brought by our scholars like Sheikh al-Albaanee. He, may Allaah have mercy upon him, offered every sincere Muslim a signpost that, individually and collectively, we need to recognize, in order to chose and then walk the correct path.[7]

> *"There will be no success for the Muslims in truly lifting and removing from themselves the state of subjugation, humiliation, and colonization from their lands, nor will any benefit be produced from their political coalitions of Islamic groups and Muslim oriented political parties, except that they fully turn and truly adhere to the authentic Sunnah.*
>
> *Moreover, that their doing so, is fully done upon the methodology of our righteous predecessors of the first three generations, may Allaah be pleased with them all, in their beliefs, in the fiqh rulings implemented from the source texts, and in their character as Muslims, not by simply remaining upon whatever the later generations of people stand upon today."*

It is a requirement that we base our way upon full Sharee'ah knowledge, and engage in what will actually benefits us, not merely engage in what is pleasing to us, Muslim organizations, our tribes, or various Muslim groups. We see that much of the confusion among Muslims about what is the correct way and methodology of living Islaam starts at the very foundations of what we understand to be our religion or 'deen'. What is specifically considered worship or 'ibaadah' within that revealed guidance that Allaah has sent us? What is actually the evidenced meaning of 'Sharee'ah' with our source texts? Is it only classical judicial codes and criminal punishments? Or it

[7] Silsilaat al-Hadeeth as-Saheehah: vol. 7 pg. 617

is only the ritual rites and yearly observances of Islaam which people practice? Sheikh Muhammad Baazmool, may Allaah preserve him, mentions in a work specifically written about the many terms and words connected to Islaam that are often misunderstood by Muslims today, what clarifies some of the confusion about the true meanings of the words 'Sharee'ah' and 'deen',[8]

"Sharee'ah: It is something commonly said among some of the people that the Sharee'ah specifically only refers to matters of ritual worship or matters of law concerning transactions which are found in the terminology used within the different sections of the books of Fiqh!!

Yet the reality is that the true meaning of Sharee'ah of the entire religion of Islaam. It is that comprehensive clear path which it is an obligation to adhere to and proceed upon with both your heart and your body. The term mutually applies to every matter related to inward correct beliefs just as it applies to what is connected to outward actions and endeavors. Look at what has been mentioned under the discussion of the term "deen", for an additional explanation of this. And the true success only comes from Allaah."

He, may Allaah preserve him, also emphasizes this essential understanding in the other referred to section related to the correct Islamic meaning of the Arabic term 'deen', stating that,[9]

"Deen: It is something commonly said among some of the people that term deen specifically refers to the rulings of matters of related to business transactions or just matters of ritual worship, and that it does not apply to issues connected to inward beliefs.

---

[8] al-Haqeeqatul Sharee'ah: pg. 110
[9] al-Haqeeqatul Sharee'ah: pg. 92-94

Yet the reality is that within the revealed source texts this term is used to encompass the entire religion of Islaam, including the areas of worship, daily business transactions, personal character, and essential inward beliefs.

*The evidence which supports this assertion is found in the long hadeeth of Jibreel. At the end of which, after the mention of emaan, Islaam, ihsaan, and some of the matters connected to the Hour of Judgement, the Prophet says, {**Indeed this was Jibreel, he came to teach you your deen, or religion.**} And in another sound varying related narration {...**That was Jibreel. He came to teach the people their deen, or religion.**} This hadeeth narration indicates clearly that the deen or religion encompasses all of these different matters....*

*...In light of what has been clarified it is only suitable to comprehensively understand and explain the words of the Prophet, may the praise and salutations of Allaah be upon him, {...**until you return to your religion**}(as authentically narrated in Sunan Abu Dawud: 3462). But as for restrictedly claiming to explain "returning to the religion" as only reviving the spirit of military Jihaad, or returning to an understanding of Islaam which simply negates some modern forms of disbelief and apostasy alone. Then clearly this is a deficiency in properly understanding the intended meaning within this hadeeth narration. What is required, in order to lift the humiliation and lowly position of the Muslim Ummah, is a true full return to our religion in our worship, in our characters, in our daily dealings, and our essential beliefs.*

So learn, oh Muslim, what is connected to emaan and its pillars, what is connected to Islaam and its pillars, what is connected to al-ihsaan and to its pillar, what knowledge is connected to belief in the Last Day, whatever that knowledge requires. Learn how to properly purify yourselves, how to perform the ritual prayer, how to complete the obligatory fasting, how to pay the obligatory zakaat charity, as well as how to permissibly buy and sell, how to get married properly and how to divorce properly...with all of these things being done in a manner and way that conforms to the guidance to the revealed Sharee'ah of Allaah, the Most Perfect and the Most High."

Every sincere Muslim admires and recognizes the beauty of the lives of the noble Companions we hear and read about from the blessed first age of Islaam, may Allaah be pleased with them all. Each of us would be pleased to see some of those same sweet fruits of living Islaam truly reflected among Muslims today. Yet without the same foundations of knowledge and understanding, that enabled their sound development, and that cultivation upon the truth found among those first generations of Islaam, we will not be blessed to be able to proceed upon the same firm path of success which they have paved and made smooth for us. That hope which we have must begin with authentic beneficial knowledge which is connected to every area of our inner and outward lives. As such, it begins with distinguishing between true worship and false worship, between knowledge and misguidance, and between religious innovation and the guidance of the Sunnah. Ibn Taymeeyah, may Allaah have mercy upon him, said,[10]

"The path of the Sunnah is distinguished by knowledge, being just, and with guidance. Whereas with innovation there is ignorance and oppression, and within it there is the following of speculations and that which leads people into error."

---

[10] Majmu'a al-Fataawaa: vol. 10 pg. 568

For that reason the verifying scholar, Sheikh Saaleh al-Fauzaan, may Allaah preserve him, has said,[11]

> *"It is beneficial knowledge which brings a good position and honor in this world and the Hereafter. It is the cause for rectification and true success in this world and the next, as opposed to ignorance. While ignorance only bring us misguidance, our true destruction, and empty arrogance."*

The acts of worship we put forth, when we stand up and say we are Muslims, must be based upon that preserved knowledge that Allaah revealed through His final Prophet and Messenger . It is through him, as the last prophet, that Allaah informed humanity fully how to fulfill that obligation of true worship that He commands from each and every one of us. Sheikh Ibn Baaz, may Allaah have mercy upon him, mentioned that gaining this knowledge is an individual obligation,[12]

> *"Therefore, what is an obligation upon the people of Islaam is that they learn and strive to understand before falling into any mistakes when performing their acts of ritual worship: such as their performance of the ritual prayers, or their fulfillment of the obligation of fasting, or their performance of the rites of Hajj, or in their undertaking of jihaad in Allaah's path, meaning before each and every one of their affairs.*
>
> *But if it is decreed that someone neglected this and only asked afterwards, about his prayer regarding something which happened in his performance of prayer or about something that happened in his establishing his fasting, then such individuals are those people whom seeking knowledge of those matters becomes obligatory upon them individually and specifically. As Allaah said,* **Ask the people of knowledge if you do not know.** *-(Surah*

[11] Sharh Manthoomat al-Ihsaa'aee: pg. 13
[12] Fataawa Series Light Upon the Path vol. 1, pg. 481-482

an-Nahl: 43) meaning before forming that worship and afterwards, before engaging in it and after doing so.

He should prepare himself and ask about the matter before embarking upon its performance, such that he equips himself with a complete preparation, such that when he proceeds to perform that act of worship he performs it upon knowledge and insight. This is what is required and this is the sound path to take."

This same reminder about striving to learn sound Sharee'ah knowledge first and foremost is also heard from Sheikh al-'Utheimeen, may Allaah have abundant mercy upon him, who stated,[13]

"I advise our brothers in Islaam that if they wish to put forth some act of worship that they learn its details before engaging in it. If is was decreed that they already performed some worship without having asked about its correct details and performed it incorrectly, then they should take the initiative now and ask about the correct way to perform it in order to fulfill the obligation they have to complete it suitably.

This is so that they do not reach the time of meeting Allaah, the Most Glorified and the Most Exalted, and they have failed to ask about the knowledge of matters which were considered obligatory upon them."

If this is the case with individual acts of worship, how important is having a sound understanding of the true meaning of worshiping Allaah alone which is the main obligation of our very lives!

---

[13] From the program 'Light Upon the Path': collection 7 program 18

Yet it is, unfortunately, a common practice today to unthinkingly place the words of this Muslim leader, that Muslim blog writer, this Muslim Youtube 'caller' or that Muslim 'intellectual' at the top of the list of good sources when either seeking to understand what is accepted worship or when being reminded and encouraged to establish aspects of it in every area of our lives. However Sheikh al-'Utheimeen, may Allaah have mercy upon him, reminds us that,[14]

> *"We do not need to search for any admonishment or reminder more effective at enlivening and inspiring our hearts than the Book of Allaah and the Sunnah.*
>
> *Rather, we have everything we need within them. As they hold the inheritance of knowledge of Muhammad. the final Messenger of Allaah, may Allaah's praise and salutations be upon him, which is sufficient and satisfying in every single area and branch of Sharee'ah knowledge and our inward and outward faith in Allaah."*

For this reason it is important to offer a reminder of what was discussed and brought forth in book one of this course series, the importance of recognizing the true fundamental sources of our religion. In that course book we asked, what are the sources from which we should take both the fundamentals and details of our religion and its purifying beliefs? The guidance of Islaam, as it was revealed, showed that, the two sources of revelation and Consensus should always be given precedence before the words of any Muslim leader, Muslim blog writer, Muslim Youtube 'caller' or Muslim 'intellectual'. Furthermore, there is an additional important tooth on the key of properly understanding the "straight path' Allah intends for us.

---

[14] Sharh al-Aqeedat al-Wasateeyah: vol. 2 pg. 183

Many scholars including, the noble scholar of hadeeth sciences from the early centuries, Haafidh Abee Haatim ar-Raazee, may Allaah have mercy upon him, made clear that the correct detailed way for every Muslim is to adhere to those foundations and original sources of Islaam, is through holding onto the transmitted understanding and practice of those guided Muslims coming before us had of them. He said,[15]

> *"Our way and what we have chosen is to follow the Messenger of Allaah, may the praise and salutations of Allaah be upon him, along with his Companions, and those who followed them in goodness. And to hold firmly to the way of those who refer to transmitted knowledge, such as Abu 'Abdullah Ahmad Ibn Hanbal."*

The first three generations of the Muslim Ummah are who correctly realized and practically implemented those foundations of knowledge. This means starting with the first generation of the Ummah, and includes all of those guided Muslims who remaining upon their unchanging way century after century. Following in their footsteps, Sheikh al-Islaam Ibn Taymeeyah, may Allaah have mercy upon him, reminds us of this same distinction of our methodology saying,[16]

> *"Our beliefs are not to be taken from me as their origin, nor taken from those who are greater and more significant than me. But they are only taken from the Book of Allaah, the Sunnah of the Messenger of Allaah, and what the Salaf, the first three generation, stood in Consensus upon."*

---

[15] Sharh Usul 'Itiqaad Ahlis-Sunnah wa al-Jamaa'ah of Imam al-Lalikaa'ee: vol. 1 pg. 180
[16] Jaame'a al-Masa'il: vol 8 pg. 183

Likewise in our century the noble Sheikh 'Abdur-Razzaq 'Abdul-Muhsin al-Badr, may Allaah preserve him, said explaining why a number of sound works about authentic beliefs are connected to scholar of the Sunnah who authored it in their titles,[17]

> *"A number of the people of knowledge authored several scholarly works related to beliefs, works which have come to be known as "The belief of so-and-so' but this designation or title is a only put forward from the specific fact that they, that specific scholar of the Sunnah, gathered it, compiled it, organized it, collected together the sound evidences supporting it, and then believed in it.*
>
> *This is in direct contrast to the people of innovation and what is attributed to them of their writing and works, that only being whatever they themselves have falsely invented and newly developed and added to the religion."*

He, in this same work which is a commentary on a sound book of beliefs, also reminds us about how numerous dangerous religious innovations which people spread actually are saying,[18]

> *"And his statement* **"The invented matters of those who are misguided..."**
>
> *"These newly invented matters and religious innovations are very numerous, they do not have any limit nor can even be counted. Yet having protection from all of them certainly lies in firmly adhering to the Book of Allaah and the Sunnah..."*

---

[17] Ta'leeq 'Alaa Sharh as-Sunnah lil Imaam al-Muzanee: pg. 46
[18] Ta'leeq 'Alaa Sharh as-Sunnah lil Imaam al-Muzanee: pg. 48

This understanding, which is the focus of this second course book, clearly distinguishes the person who gives attention and focusing on striving in worship upon the pure Sunnah, from those today who chose a specific Sufee "tareeqah" and path. Some Muslims seeking inner purity and closeness to Allaah, wrongly adopt whatever practices the scholars of their specific "tareeqah" have developed in the later and modern centuries. Yet Sheikh Ibn Baaz, may Allaah have mercy upon him, when asked by someone, how a Muslim, should be in relation to the Sufees and their practices in his land, explained clearly the difference between the Sufees and revealed Islaam,[19]

> *"Those well known groups from the Sufees, are newly developed and newly innovated groups which emerged within the history of the Muslim Ummah. Moreover, they have many different types and levels of innovation which they have wrongly attributed to the religion. Some of them have matters of religious innovation that have reached the critical level of major association of others with Allaah, which removes someone from the religion, while others among them have innovations that are blameworthy but of a lesser degree of misguidance.*
>
> *As such, my advice to you, oh questioner, is that you do not connect yourself to them, or any of their groups or tareeqahs, nor be deceived by their subtle claims, nor be someone who joins with them in their innovated activities. Instead, you should follow and adhere to the Sunnah, and hold firmly to its guidance, which Allaah has legislated for humanity. Meaning that guidance which is clearly found within the Book of Allaah and the Sunnah of the Messenger of Allaah, may the praise and salutations of Allaah be upon him. Additionally, you should direct your questions about the religion, to*

---

[19] From the Program Nur Alaa Dharb- light upon the Path - binbaz.org.sa: Fatwa: no. 18019

those people of knowledge who are well-known to be upon sound beliefs, and to be steadfast upon the path and methodology of the people of the Sunnah and the Jamaa'ah...

...meaning those individuals who are known for their Sharee'ah knowledge and merit by the rest of the scholars, ask them and benefit from them. This is how is it suitable that you proceed.

But as for standing with the people of Sufism, then no. As they have been overwhelmed by false beliefs and ways innovated into the religion, as well as superstitious practices. These new practices which they themselves have developed, and then chosen to establish as their own system of "purification of the soul" have no clear detailed basis in the pure revealed Sharee'ah from Allaah.

Furthermore, as mentioned some of their innovations are misguidance that reaches the level of major association with Allaah, which is disbelief in Islaam, such as their directing some forms of worship towards the dead righteous Muslims, seeking the help and assistance of intercession of deceased worshipers within their graves, and similar matters. This is seen in the supplications made by them at the grave of al-Badawee, and their seeking the assistance of al-Badawee, or of al-Husayn, may Allaah be pleased with him, at what is (claimed to be) his grave, and other new practices similar to this. All of these types of actions are from the dangerous higher level of directing worship to others besides Allaah. Similar to this is their religiously walking around these grave sites and their building elevated decorated tombs over these graves which people proceed around. All of these actions are tremendous matters of wrongdoing and sin.

The only legitimate form of walking around something as an act of worship, is circumambulating around the Ka'aba. Those who walk around a grave or a raised tomb or something similar, are performing an act of circumambulation, which is worship, directed towards other than Allaah. It direct it towards the occupant in that grave or towards the one who within that raised tomb, or even to the tomb itself, supplicating to it and having a belief in its benefit for people. All of this reaches the level of major disbelief, and we ask Allaah for ourselves both health and wellbeing in our practice of our religion.

Therefore it is an obligation upon you, to investigate and look closely at what you consider your religion. You should put forth significant effort in reading and contemplating the noble Qur'aan, along with reciting it. Also strive in learning the pure Sunnah, focusing on it and giving it attention. Strive to memorize works such as "Bulugh al-Maram" or "Umdaat (al-Ahkam) in order that they benefit you. This should be undertaken along with asking questions to those scholars who are well-known to have sound beliefs and to live their lives in a correct praiseworthy way from among the people of knowledge….

…ask those who have Sharee'ah knowledge from those known to have understanding in your land, meaning those who have knowledge of the Sunnah and are separated from the people of Sufism and the extreme practices they engage in at the graves of the righteous. Since this itself, is a sign of those who are truly the people of the Sunnah. Such people are those who are far away from those involved with Sufism, and those who have fallen in to these extreme practices done at the graves of the deceased righteous.

This characteristic is itself a sign that a scholar is from the people of the Sunnah, meaning that he calls to the Noble Qur'aan and the pure Sunnah, and he warns against engaging in forms of worship at graves and against seeking the assistance of the deceased within graves, and all similar matters of misguidance. They are those who distance themselves from the various religious innovations of the Sufees. This is a sign of a scholar who is an individual firmly adhering to the Sunnah. I ask Allaah to grant all of us guidance and true success."

Sheikh Saaleh al-Fauzaan, may Allaah preserve him, in his precise refutation of the al-Rafa'ee, a caller to Sufism, says directly quoting ar-Rafa'ee's own misguiding statements,[20]

"His statement, [Certainly, whenever we are speaking about Sufism and calling to it, we intend by that the Sufism practiced by Imaam ar-Rafaa'ee, al-Jilanee, ad-Dusuqee, ash-Shandhalee, and an-Naqshabandee. We do not mean the extreme Sufism of Ibn Arabee....]

We say to him, Sufism in its entirety is an innovated way. Even if some aspects of it are of a lesser degree of misguidance than others, then the more diluted aspects of falsehood eventually lead to involvement in what are its more severe and dangerous forms of misguidance. This is something clearly witnessed and is a recognized reality seen today among those attached to Sufism.

Moreover, this is the general way of lesser practices of religious innovation, that they eventually lead to worse forms of misguidance than that initial lesser misguidance.

*Certainly, the Prophet, may Allaah's praise and salutations be upon him, clearly said, {**Adhere to my Sunnah and the sunnah of my rightly guided Khaleefahs after me.***

---

[20] Taken from the main website of Sheikh al-Fauzaan-.alfawzan.af.org.sa no. 2357

Hold firmly to it with your molar teeth. Be warned against newly emerging matters in the religion, as every innovation in the religion is misguidance...} As Sufism, as a methodology, is something newly invented and later developed within the practice of Islaam, therefore it is misguidance and something wrong."

...He stated, [If a Sunnee Muslim engages in practices of Sufism is he then seen as a wrongdoer?!]

I say, yes, anyone who embraces Sufism has chosen to innovate in Islaam, and whoever chooses to innovate in Islaam is a wrongdoer.

The one who is considered Sunnee, if he knowingly embraces Sufism, he no longer remains a Sunnee, meaning someone proceeding upon the Sunnah, rather he becomes someone connected to innovation.

ar-Rafa'ee also says about those who oppose his opinion about Sufism. [They are only the students of Ibn Baaz, and are only people upon blind following without using their intellects. They come from the same mold as him, and have simply been brainwashed.]

I say, as for their being the students of Sheikh Ibn Baaz, then this is only an honor for them, may Allaah have mercy upon him. He was an Imaam, a distinguished scholar, from among the leading scholars of the people of the Sunnah. But as for you, please make clear to us, who you are from among the students of the acknowledged scholars?? As for your statement, [...without using their intellects] then we say to you, the religion is foremost based upon revealed evidences coming from the Book of Allaah and the Sunnah, not merely our intellects.

As for your statement, [...and have simply been brainwashed.] Then we say yes, their brains have been washed clean of invented superstitions and baseless fallacies, and all praise is due to Allah for that."

But then, we should ask, what exactly is the way this noble Sheikh, and others like him from the people of knowledge who completely reject Sufism, believe a Muslim purifies his soul. How can a Muslim strive to become someone who fears Allaah both inwardly and outwardly? What is the way taken by those who reject the claimed [good innovations] of the Sufees. What is the alternative to the new practices developed by those leading Sufees who some wrongly consider "close associates" of Allaah? This is also made clear by Sheikh al-Fauzaan, may Allaah preserve him, when he was asked, **"How can a person come to be someone who is conscious of his Lord inwardly and outwardly?"** He replied,[21]

"He becomes someone who is conscious of his Lord by having fear of Allaah, the Most Glorified and the Most Exalted. This has several means or causes leading to it among which are: frequently reciting the Qur'aan, frequently verbally engaging in ritual remembrance of Allaah, the Most Glorified and the Most Exalted, and through spending time with the people of righteousness. Each of these are matters which lead to a person developing the consciousness of Allaah, fearing Him, the Most Glorified and the Most Exalted.

He should not neglect the remembrance of Allaah, nor the recitation of the Qur'aan, not those affirmed statements of remembrance that the Sunnah says which are to be said specifically during the daytime or the evening time. Moreover, before all of this he must preserve and maintain the performance of every matter Allah has obligated upon him as Muslim. He must preserve the

[21] From the website alfawzan.af.org.sa no.15903

performance of the five obligatory prayers at the required times, and if an adult male, in congregation, with all of this upon true sincerity of doing it for the sake of Allaah, the Most Glorified and the Most Exalted."

True purification of our beliefs, statements, thoughts, ideas, and behaviors is only accomplished through the Sunnah, proceeding upon the Sunnah, as guided by the Sunnah. Moreover, we do not abandon matters from the Sunnah, such as stressing the importance of dhikr throughout our daily lives as Muslims, simply because the people of misguidance have hijacked aspects or some practices from it. Sheikh Muhammad Baazmool, may Allaah preserve him said,[22]

"It is not from the methodology of the first three esteemed generations of the Muslim Ummah to hide or conceal a legitimate aspect of the Sunnah simply because some of the people of innovation have connected that matter to themselves. Yet this is something we have seen repeatedly from some of our brothers. I recall one of our brothers was known to be from the direct lineage of the Prophet's household, but he chose not to reveal that and instead concealed it. So I discussed this with him, and he responded saying, you must excuse me but that practice is something often brought forward by the people of Sufism or is something they newly concocted in this area!

I also recall that one my scholars, had specific chains of narrations for transmitting works of knowledge and has commendations for proficiency in specific areas of Sharee'ah knowledge, but he did not make that publicly apparent. So I discussed this with him, and he similarly responded saying, you must excuse me but this practice is something done by the people of Sufism. However, I discussed the abandonment of that with him and after some time, all praise is due to Allaah, he made

[22] From the Facebook page of Sheikh Muhammad Ibn 'Umar Baazmool

public both his specific chains of narrations and his commendations for different areas of knowledge. He also further granted me scholastic commendations from among those specific commendations which had been given to him, may Allaah protect and preserve him.

Likewise, when I have previous spoken about having knowledge related contests or similar activities among people, some have said to me that this is from the ways some of the groups of partisanship. Yet I reply that we are more rightfully deserving to whatever truly comes from the Sunnah of the Messenger of Allaah, may Allaah's praise and salutations be upon him than them! Therefore do not abandon matters from the affirmed practices of the Chosen Last Messenger simply because of what is done by the people of innovation!"

This second course book, by Allaah's permission, may help some of us as Muslims to better understand the true danger or the "bitter poison within the sweetness of honey" of the claim of continually bringing [good innovation] into Islaam. These innovations are done by some Muslims in order, as they wrongly claim, to complement and enrich the guidance which has come from our beloved Messenger, may the praise and salutations of Allaah be upon him. There are many today who openly advocate and call to the false belief that the meaning of ritual worship in our religion is "flexible" and "open". They strive to spread that belief that [good innovations] can be continually added to the original practices of the first Muslims within Islaam. In their understanding of the religion Allaah revealed and perfected, fundamentally new beliefs and practices, are normal as it "develops" and "grows" like other religions!

Yet the preserved source texts of the Qur'aan and Sunnah continually and repeatedly contradict them. Since these are new matters which the Prophet, may the praise and salutations of Allaah be upon him, never practiced himself nor ever called others to.

For this reason, another focus of this second course book, based upon the beginning of text of Usul as-Sunnah of Imaam Ahmad, may Allaah have mercy upon him, is to gain a basic overview of religious innovation and what the source texts, generally and specifically, inform us about its nature and danger. Additionally, I have tried to bring some authentic statements showing how the early Muslims, after the death of our Prophet, may the praise and salutations of Allaah be upon him, understood the meaning of innovation within Islaam. Did they hold it to be something sometimes good and beneficial adding to the good of Islaam? Or did they believe it was something avoided by the one adhering to the Sunnah as our Prophet commanded?

There is little question that in the current century Shaytaan, and those from his party, work diligently to spread and revive misconceptions about the true nature of religious innovation, as is seen today among many confused stumbling callers to Islaam. This is one reason why we see our modern verifying scholars, the true inheritors of the Messenger, due to their love of Allaah as their Lord, their love of the Prophet Muhammad as their Messenger, and from their love of Islaam as their deen, continually struggling to drive people towards the light of the Sunnah and away from the misguidance of religious innovation. When we look at the efforts of the guided scholars who adhered to the Sunnah over the centuries we find that in each and every century scholars held and acted upon the belief mentioned by Sheikh al-'Utheimeen, may Allaah have mercy upon him, that, [23]

---

[23] Majmu'a al-Fataawa Sheikh Muhammad Ibn Saaleeh al-'Utheimeen: vol. 2 pg.

"Preserving the Sunnah is by defending it and refuting those misconceptions of the people of innovation."

We see this implemented by the sheikh himself, as Sheikh al-'Utheimeen was someone vigorous in his efforts of defending the Sunnah. He, may Allaah have abundant mercy upon him, was someone who strove against the people of innovation in many ways and in different areas of knowledge, whether that was correct beliefs, methodology, explanations of the Qur'aan, or fiqh and its principles. In the following section we see that he, may Allaah have mercy upon him, was asked a question about examples of innovation and their effect upon the Ummah by a Muslim from Jordan. Sheikh al-'Utheimeen's response provides us with both the core transmitted principles to apply as well as a sharp criterion. We should use this criterion when looking at the claims, so often made about new acts of ritual worship, called to by the people of innovation past and present. He, may Allaah have mercy upon him, stated in his response to this question,[24]

"... 'However, I will give the questioner a basic principle to use regarding any new matter brought forth which the people ritually worship Allaah through, whether from a belief of the heart, or a statement of the tongue, or an action of the body. We say to the one advocating that matter: you are considered an innovator until you bring to us the evidence that what you are calling to is legislated in the Sharee'ah.

Hold firmly to this principle, oh questioner! Any person who ritually worships Allaah with any new matter from a belief of the heart, or statement of the tongue, or an action of the body, and says [This is legislated.] Then we say to them: you are considered an innovator until you bring to us the evidence from the Book of Allaah, or from

---
143
[24] Nur Alaa Dharb: vol. 1 pg. 443

the Sunnah of the Messenger, or from the statements of the Companions, or evidence that the Muslim Ummah has come to stand in Consensus upon this, which indicates that what you are calling to is legislated in the Sharee'ah.

Because the foundation of the religion is something legislated by revelation. In addition, the basic principle in acts of ritual worship is that they are prohibited until the evidence is established that an act is something specifically legislated.

*It is for this reason that our 'Imaam', our model, and example the Messenger, may the praise and salutations of Allaah be upon him, gave us a principle to implement, saying {...**So stick to what you know from my Sunnah and the Sunnah of the rightly guided caliphs. And beware of newly invented matters, as every newly invented matter is an innovation, and every innovation is a going astray.**}[25] He also provided us with another principle when he said, {**The one who does a deed which is not in accordance with our way, it is rejected.**} meaning rejected back to the one who did it, since it is an unsupported religious innovation.*

This means that if someone says to you:

[The one who sends salaam on the Prophet, may the praise and salutations of Allaah be upon him, a thousand times, every day and night, will have written for them such and such in rewards with Allaah.]

We say: Bring your evidence, and if you cannot then clearly you are an innovator."

---

[25] Narrated in Jaame'a at-Tirmidhee: 2676/ Sunan Ibn Maajah: 42/ & Musnad Imaam Ahmad: 16692, 16694, 16695/ and within other collection- on the authority of al-'Irbaadh Ibn Saareeyah. It was declared authentic by Sheikh al-Albaanee in Silsilat al-Hadeeth as-Saheehah: 937 as well as in others of his books. Additionally Sheikh Muqbil declared it authentic in al-Jaame' al-Saheeh: 3249.

If someone further says to you:

[The one who recites the Surah "Say He is Allaah the one." a thousand times, will have written for them such and such in rewards with Allaah.]

We say: 'Bring your evidence, and if you cannot then clearly you are an innovator.'"

If they then reply about the first claim: [But sending salaams on the Prophet, may the praise and salutations of Allaah be upon him, is an action legislated at any time.]

We say: What you have said is generally true, but then why have you wrongly restricted it to specifically be said a thousand times! Where is your evidence that this is correct?"

Similarly, if they responded (about the other claim) saying [But the surah "Say He is Allaah the one." is equal to one third of the Qur'aan, and reciting it is a legislated action.]

We say: What you have said is generally true, but who, from those upon guidance, restricted or called to saying it a thousand times! Where is your evidence that this is correct?"

And so forth. This basic principle, all praise is due to Allaah, and satisfying, and very clear....

....So pay close attention oh my brother the questioner, and let everyone we hears my words also pay close attention to this subtle point which is used by the people of innovation, and those upon newly introduced religious practices, which is used by them to confuse and disguise matters.

> *When they say, [This matter is legislated, or about this matter there is nothing actually prohibiting it.] Then one should respond, "Rather the Prophet, may the praise and salutations of Allaah be upon him, said, about all such matters, {**Every religious innovation is misguidance.**}*

It is through adhering to these clear simple principles that our Prophet gave us, and which he taught to his Companions, and which the people of guidance in every age, both scholars and general Muslims, have come to always be satisfied with the Sunnah, as a revealed way of guidance, holding it as sufficient to be successful in life. Moreover, it is through these principles that they have always been dominant, in both knowledge and living authentic practice, over the weak confusing arguments and misguided practices of those who deceptively claim [We have a thousand years of scholarship supporting good innovation!]. The people of the Sunnah can reply to them, with strength and satisfaction, that they have twenty three years of the life, guidance, and Sunnah of best of humanity, and that this is sufficient for every Muslim. The people of the Sunnah can say that they are pleased to stand and struggle to raise their families upon the simplicity of the clear preserved perfected Islaam, without the need for the claimed "improvements" and "upgrades" of new innovations the innovators will always eagerly offer. One of the eminent scholars from the noble Companions, 'Abdullah Ibn 'Abbaas, may Allaah be pleased with him and his father, said, "*The Prophet, may the praise and salutations of Allaah be upon him, was asked, 'Which religion is most beloved to Allaah, the Most Glorified and the Most Exalted?' He replied, {The simple Haneefeeyah.}*[26]

---

[26] Silsilaatul Ahadeeth as-Saheehah: no. 881

For this reason, Sheikh al-Mu'alamee al-Yamaanee, may Allaah have mercy upon him, said,[27]

"Those who have proceeded steadfastly upon the path of Islaam established by the first generations of the Ummah have continually remained as those victorious over the innovators in the religion."

Likewise, the guiding scholar Sheikh Muhammad 'Alee Ferkous,[28] in the land of Algeria, may Allaah the Most

[27] Aathaar al-Mu'alamee vol.4 pg. 165
[28] By Allaah's mercy, it is one of the blessing coming from the steadfast scholars, known for clarity in beliefs and the methodology of Islaam, that they identify for the Muslim Ummah generally, and for those striving to adhere to the Sunnah specifically, not only who are the scholars the Muslims should take their deen from, but also their level among the people of knowledge of the saved victorious sect present in every age. From among the various general and detailed praises and commendations of some of the scholars of Salafeeyah for Sheikh Ferkous are the following:

1) Sheikh Muhammad Ibn Ramzaan al-Haajaree, may Allaah preserve him, said during his explanation of the book "Akhlaaq al-Ulema" or The Character of the Scholars, held of the eleventh day of Sha'baan in the year 1439, about Sheikh Muhammad 'Alee Ferkous, may Allaah preserve him,

" *...There are those who are referred back to. In Algeria, one who is referred back to is Sheikh Ferkous, just as here in Saudi one who is referred back to is Sheikh al-Fauzaan. As he is a scholar, yes.*"

Several years ago Dr. Fawaad 'Ataa' Allaah, conveyed that, "Last night I attended the lesson of Sheikh Muhammad al-Haajaree, may Allaah the Most High preserve him, of his explanation of the book "Usul as-Sittah" by Sheikh Muhammad Ibn 'Abdul-Wahaab, may Allaah have mercy upon him. Sheikh Muhammad al-Haajaree, may Allaah reward him with good, said about Sheikh Ferkous, may Allaah preserve him,

"*This man, Allaah has given him abundance in knowledge and in physical strength. As I previously meet him two or three times during the Hajj season.*"

2) Sheikh Muhammad Ibn 'Abdul-Wahaab al-'Aqeel, may Allaah preserve his stated,
"*In the name of Allaah the Most Gracious, the Most Merciful*
All praise is due to Allaah Lord of all the worlds. May the prayers and good mention of Allaah by upon our Prophet Muhammad, the one sent as a mercy to all the worlds, and also be upon his household and all his Companions.
As for what follows:
*Allah the Most High said, "Ask the people of knowledge if you do not know." And the Prophet, may the praise and salutations of Allaah be upon him said, {**The scholars are the inheritors of the prophets.**} The Imaam Taawoos Ibn Kaysaan, may Allaah have mercy upon him said, "It is from the guidance of the Sunnah to honor and respect four: the scholar, the parent, the Muslim ruler, and the elderly Muslim."*
From among the cultivating scholars who are known and distinguished by abundant knowledge, verification and knowledge based writings, strength upon the truth, and steadfastness upon the Sunnah, is the guiding scholar, the Sheikh Muhammad 'Alee Ferkous, the senior scholar of the people of knowledge in Algeria, He is someone from who those seeking knowledge and the guidance of Sharee'ah rulings in that land turn to. So I advise that you benefit from this significant scholar, understanding his right as a scholar, and defend his

High preserve him, also stated this important fact clearly, [29]

*"The people of the Sunnah, those who follow the way of the righteous predecessors of the Ummah, they do not conceal their way, and their statements upon the truth are apparent and evident. They have never turned away, in any of the past ages, from making the truth apparent and explaining the reality of those people who have turned away from guidance and neglected it. Indeed, the Messenger of Allaah, may Allaah's praise and salutations be upon him, said, {**There will not cease to remain a group from my Ummah clearly apparent upon the truth. Those who abandon them will not harm them, until the time of Allaah final judgement comes, and they remain in that state.** }(narrated in Saheeh Muslim)."*

honor. This is what is apparent to me about him, and I do not purify anyone over what Allaah knows of them. May the praise and salutations of Allaah be upon our Prophet, his household, and all his Companions.

Written by Muhammad Ibn 'Abdul-Wahaab Ibn Muhammad al-'Aqeel, on the second day of the month of Allaah al-Muharram in the year 1440 of the Hijrah of the Prophet."

3) Sheikh Sulaymaan ar-Ruhaylee, may Allaah preserve him, as recording in an audio file in his voice, said,

"...*Alhamdulillah, today there is no excuse. Look, the lectures of the scholars are broadcast directly live. They can be found on various internet sites, they can be found also on Youtube, so they are available. The scholars of the Sunnah, all praise is due to Allah, now have a good presence among the people. It is true they aren't found in the websites of these Muslim political movements and parties, but certainly their presence elsewhere is very apparent.*

So I say, may Allaah have mercy upon you, that making the Sunnah distinct, and making its people distinct is a Sharee'ah obligation. It is not permissible that these misguided false concepts be brought forward and allowed to emerge, as in reality they are only from the weakening of true guidance that will never result in any good for the Muslims."

Some of those standing with the sheikh then speak, and one questioner asks him, "**Our sheikh, regarding Sheikh Ferkous, in Algeria, what is your advice concerning him?**" Sheikh ar-Ruhaylee replied,

"*I should offer advice about Sheikh Ferkous?? In fact Sheikh Ferkous is greater and more knowledgable than me.*"

4) Sheikh Sulaymaan Ibn 'Abdullah Abaa al-Khayl, may Allaah preserve him, in his book "Salafeeyah, It's Reality, Principles, & Position Towards Takfeer", said, "...*And the scholar of fiqh and the fundamentals of the religion Sheikh Muhammad 'Alee Ferkous al-Jazaa'ree, may Allaah grant him success, said in his treatise 'The Personal Rectification of the Muslim Individual, is the Foundation of the Steadfastness of His Religion & of the Rectification of the Muslim Ummah', "As for the expression Wahaabeeyah, then it is generally used to oppose what is the call to the truth by the people of desires and innovation..."*"

[29] Monthly Statement 43 from Sheikh Ferkous

The Most Important Achievement We Can Accomplish

It is important for every Muslim to know that, the discussion of the true meaning, importance, and actual boundaries of worship is something directly connected to fully understanding our purpose in life and how to live it. Yet many Muslims today unknowingly have significant gaps and misconceptions that weaken this essential foundation for their success in both worlds. After struggling to turn back towards Allaah to try to live a life of sincere worship, there are few diseases that are as harmful as not properly understanding what is actually true worship in Islaam. Sheikh Muhammad Ibn Saaleh al-'Utheimeen, may Allaah have mercy upon him, said,[30]

> *"What is important, oh my brothers, is that we are truly concerned with reviving, within the very souls of the people, the spirit of focusing upon importance of worshipping Allaah alone, meaning that tawheed which realizes Allaah's right to be worshipped alone.*
>
> *Such that a person's primary goal becomes seeking the pleasure of Allaah and success in the next life in how he conducts and proceeds in all of his affairs: in his acts of ritual worship, as reflected in his character, within his everyday transactions, in all of the different areas of his life.*
>
> *This is what is important: that a Muslim's central goal and main objective, meaning his true hope and aspiration, and his wishing to return and meet Allaah, the Most Exalted, the Most Magnificent, all be through realizing this matter of worship, and specifically this obligation of directing worship to Allaah alone.*

---

[30] Majmu'a ar-Risa'il Sheikh al-'Utheimeen: vol. 7 pg. 351

Indeed, his fulfilling this worship achieves for each worshipper of Allaah who engages in it the true success in both this world and the next."

Reviving that spirit is only accomplished through learning, implementing, spreading beneficial Sharee'ah knowledge as much are we are truly able to with our many deficiencies, as well as warning against the traps of Shaytaan, found in all the various forms of apparent and subtle misguidance. As Imaam as-Sa'adee, may Allaah have mercy upon him, stated,[31]

"Every matter of knowledge which contains direction and guidance towards the path of goodness, and warns against the path of evil and wrongdoing, or is a means that directs towards either of these two, then certainly it is considered beneficial knowledge."

I close the preface to this second course book with an important reminder from a scholar who was an influential noble caller, who clarified, the beliefs, worship, and the clear methodology of Islaam, Sheikh Zayd al-Madkhalee. He, may Allaah have abundant mercy upon him, said,[32]

"There will not come any year except that it is worse in ways, than the years which preceded it.

This is due to what appears of people engaging in sins, the emergence of different trials, from the harmful love of wealth and the following of desires, and the appearance of a reduced concern for good and fostering the presence of what is good among people.

---

[31] Tayseer al-Lateef al-Manaan: pg. 257
[32] From his explanation of al-Adaab al-Mufrad: pgs. 139-140

As such, it is obligatory that an individual, take a lesson and sincerely be reminded that nothing will truly benefit him other than what he has been put forward for Allaah's sake. Meaning only what his own hands put forward for Allaah of righteous actions, from whatever has been required of us, whether from obligations or recommended matters, as well as his leaving whatever matters have been forbidden.

So prepare for your meeting with Allaah, the Blessed and the Most High. As that meeting is close, no matter how long your life is, the meeting with Allaah is close."

I ask Allaah, Glorified and Exalted, to place me and every Muslim and Muslimah upon the path of beneficial knowledge and righteous actions, and to enable us to walk in that truly successful path just as our pious predecessors did, making our knowledge a proof for us and not against us. May the praise and salutations of Allaah be upon the Messenger of Allaah, his household, his Companions, and all those who followed his guidance until the Day of Judgement. And all praise is due to Allaah alone, Lord of all the worlds.

Abu Sukhailah Khalil Ibn-Abelahyi al-Amreekee
Yawm al-Jumu'ah - the fifteenth day of the month Of Dhul-Hijjah
In the year one thousand four hundred and forty
Of the Hijrah of the Chosen Messenger
Allaah's praise and salutations be upon him.

[Corresponding to August 16th, 2019 C.E.]

(1)

GUIDANCE TO WORSHIP CORRECTLY COMES FROM ALLAAH ALONE

Sheikh Muhammad Ibn Saaleh al-'Utheimeen, may Allaah have mercy upon him

The noble sheikh, may Allaah have abundant mercy upon him,

*"In this sitting[1] we will open it with the explanation of the remainder of Surah Al-Layl where Allaah, the Blessed and the Most High said, ❧ **Truly! Ours it is (to give) guidance, And truly, unto Us (belong) the last (Hereafter) and the first (this world).** ❧-(Surah Al-Layl: 12-13) He, the Most Glorified and the Most Exalted, stated ❧ **Truly! Ours it is (to give) guidance.** ❧-(Surah Al-Layl: 12)*

*Within the statement is the necessity from Allaah, the Most Glorified and the Most Exalted, that He explain to the creation that which will guide them to their Lord and Creator. And what is intended by guidance here is: The guidance of explaining and directing, and Allaah, the Most High necessitated upon Himself this explanation, in order that his creation, which has a choice, would not have any justification in front of Allaah for rejecting His path. This is similar to the statement of Allaah, the Most High, ❧ **Verily, We have inspired you (O Muhammad) as We inspired Nuh (Noah) and the Prophets after him** ❧-(Surah An-Nisa': 163) Continuing on until His statement, ❧ **....messengers as bearers of good news as well as of warning in order that mankind should have no plea against Allaah after the Messengers. And Allaah is Ever All Powerful, All Wise.** ❧-(Surah An-Nisa': 165) So this matter is concluded and completed my brothers! It is not possible for the intellect of Allaah's creation to discern and determine what is complete guidance by itself, for this reason it is necessary that Allaah, the Most Glorified and the Most Exalted, explain His true way*

---
[1] Open Door Gatherings: vol.3 pg. 76

of guidance to humanity. ❧ **Truly! Ours it is (to give) guidance.** ❧ *-(Surah Al-Layl: 12)*

As such, know that guidance is of two distinct types:

Firstly, that true guidance of the heart to be upon and follow the truth. This type is not possible for anyone to give except Allaah.

Secondly, the guidance of directing towards understanding and comprehend what is the truth. This is something which may come from Allaah and may come from the direction of some of His creation, and by this meaning the messengers and their inheritors from among the scholars.

This is, as Allaah has said to His prophet, may Allaah's praise and salutation be upon him and his family, ❧ **And certainly, you (O Muhammad) call them to a Straight Path (true religion Islamic Monotheism).** ❧ *-(Surah Al-Mu'minun: 73)*

But as for the complete guidance to be truly successful in this life, then no one grants this except Allaah. No one else has ability give anyone final success to be upon goodness. Just as Allaah, the Most High says: ❧ **Verily! You (O Muhammad) guide not whom you like, but Allaah guides whom He wills. And He knows best those who are the guided.** ❧ *-(Surah Al-Qasas: 56)*

For this reason when we look and consider this noble verse: ❧ **Truly! Ours it is (to give) guidance.** ❧ *-(Surah Al-Layl: 12) We understand that truly Allaah, the Most High, has explained and clarified every matter of guidance. He has explained what it is required from true beliefs that people must have, what acts of worship it is required that they perform, what type of character they should all have, how they should be guided in their* *everyday affairs, and what they should stay away from and all these different areas of life.*

This is even to the degree, that the Companion Abu Dharr, may Allaah be pleased with him, said, **"Indeed the messenger of Allaah, may Allaah's praise and salutation be upon him and his family, died, but there is not a single bird moving its wings in the sky except that he mentioned to us about it some aspect of knowledge."** *Similarly one man from among those who associated others with Allaah in worship said to the noble Companion Salmaan al-Faarsee, "Your prophet teaches you even how to relieve yourself? And he replied,* **"Yes, he instructed us even how to properly relieve ourselves."** *By this meaning, what are the manners that a person should have, when relieving himself of bodily waste. This is something which the Prophet, may Allaah's praise and salutation be upon him and his family, taught to the Muslim Ummah. Moreover this understanding is something which is supported by the statement of Allaah, the Most High,* ❦ **This day, those who disbelieved have given up all hope of your religion, so fear them not, but fear Me. This day, I have perfected your religion for you, completed My Favor upon you, and have chosen for you Islaam as your religion.** ❦ *-(Surah Al-Ma'idah: 3)"*

This understanding of how Allaah's guidance reaches us is directly connected to the comprehensive meaning of worship found among the leading scholars who proceeding upon the Sunnah in every age and century. Their definition includes acts of ritual worship, as well as those acts of custom, which support and facilitate proceeding upon the straight path, that are done seeking Allaah's pleasure in conformance to the guidelines of the Sharee'ah. There is tremendous benefit in the scholars' explanations about this true meaning of worship. This is since the subject of 'ibaadah or worship is not only central to distinguishing Islaam from the other religions, it is also central to distinguishing the people of the Sunnah from among the many the misguided sects of innovation throughout history. There are numerous sects that have developed within the Muslim Ummah, who to varying degrees, have adopted an path of innovation and religious evolution in both their fundamental understanding, specific beliefs, and essential practices of Islaam.

The importance of guidance and an affirmation of the general comprehensive meaning of worship is also reflected in the authentic explanation and commentary of Surah al-Kaafiroon. The following is an explanation of this important surah also from Sheikh al-'Utheimeen, may Allaah have mercy upon him. This surah is central to understanding the foundation of what differentiates the proper understanding and practice of worship in Islaam which distinguishes those people those who embrace it, from its opposite. Sheikh al-'Utheimeen, may Allaah have mercy upon him, states,

"In the name of Allaah, the Most Gracious, the Most Merciful

1. Say (O Muhammad) to these Mushrikoon and Kaafirun): "O Al-Kaafirun (disbelievers in Allaah, in His Oneness, in His Angels, in His Books, in His Messengers, in the Day of Resurrection, and in Al-Qadr, etc.)"

2. "I worship not that which you worship,"

3. "Nor will you worship that which I worship."

4. "And I shall not worship that which you are worshipping."

5. "Nor will you worship that which I worship."

6. "To you be your religion, and to me my religion (Islamic Monotheism)" -(Surah al-Kaafirun: 1-6)

This surah is one of the two surahs connected to sincerity and purity of worship. This specific surah of sincerity begins with ❁ *1. Say (O Muhammad to these Mushrikoon and Kaafirun): "O Al-Kaafirun (disbelievers in Allaah, in His Oneness, in His Angels, in His Books, in His Messengers, in the Day of Resurrection, and in Al-Qadr, etc.)"* ❁While the second surah of sincerity and purity of worship begins with ❁ *1. Say (O Muhammad: "He is Allaah, (the) One.* ❁.

The Prophet, may Allaah's praise and salutations be upon him, usually recited these two surahs in those non-obligatory prayers performed around the period of fajr, maghreb, and done after performing tawwaaf around the Ka'ba. This was due to what they contain of sincerity and purity of worship being directed to Allaah, the Most Glorified and the Most Exalted, alone, as well as what is found within them in the surah that begins, ❁ *1. Say "He is Allaah, (the) One.*❁, meaning Surah Al-Ikhlaas, of praising him and mentioning His perfect attributes.

The verse ❁ *1. Say (O Muhammad to these Mushrikoon and Kaafirun)*❁ *"O Al-Kaafirun -disbelievers..."* means to call out to them openly and address them saying *"O Al-Kaafirun -disbelievers..."* This encompasses every form of disbelief in Allaah, whether that applies to those who associate others with Allaah in worship as was done before the revelation of the final message of Islaam, or applies to those upon the currently held religion of the Jews, or applies to those upon currently held religion of the Christian, or applies to to the communists, or applies to those who hold other ideologies other than these mentioned.

In relation to every single disbeliever, it is required that you address him within your heart, and possibly with your tongue if you are in their actual presence, to declare yourself free from them generally in addition to that false worship that they offer and engage in towards other than Allaah.

❁ *1. Say "O Al-Kaafirun (disbelievers in Allaah, in His Oneness, in His Angels, in His Books, in His Messengers, in the Day of Resurrection, and in Al-Qadr,) 2. I worship not that which you worship 3. Nor will you worship that which I worship. 4. And I shall not worship that which you are worshipping. 5. Nor will you worship that which I worship.*❁ Here each verse is repeated twice, one after the other preceding verse.

❁ *2. "I worship not that which you worship" I do not worship those whom you worship,*❁ meaning worshipping false objects of worship. ❁ *5. "Nor will you worship that which I worship.*❁ meaning He, Allaah, whom the Muslim worships.

Additionally,❁ *that*❁ in the statement:❁ *that which that which I worship"* has the meaning of "who" because the unstated noun refers back to Allaah, as such this has the expressed meaning "whom I worship" ❁ *"I worship not that which you worship, 5. Nor will you worship that which I worship.*❁ As such meaning "I, the Muslim, will not worship your false objects of worship, and you those who disbelieve in Islaam, will not truly worship Allaah."

Allaah says, ❁ *4. "And I shall not worship that which you are worshipping. 5. "Nor will you worship that which I worship.* ❁-(Surah al-Kaafirun: 4-5)

Certainly, some people have wrongly supposed that this repetition is intended to merely emphasize and reinforce the general overall meaning, but this is not the case since the wording and formation of the sentence is actually different in the two related verses, the first states ❧ *2. "I worship not that which you worship* ❧ and the second comes as ❧ *4. "And I shall not worship that which you are worshipping.* ❧ both the words "*Aabid*" and "*Aabidoon*" in the second sentences are nouns unlike the words used in the first two verses. Whereas, what is seen in actual cases of linguistic repetition which would convey emphasis, is that the second repeated sentence is the generally the same as the first sentence it is emphasizing. For this reason the offered explanation that these second similar verses are simply for emphasis is weak in the evidence that supports this view. If that is the case, then what is actually intended by this repetition of the second two similar verses?

Some of the scholars have stated that the verse: ❧ *2. "I worship not that which you worship* ❧ meaning in the present time or today, whereas the verse ❧ *4. "And I shall not worship that which you are worshipping.* ❧ meaning never in the future. Therefore ❧ *4. "I worship not that which you worship* ❧ refer to the current of time. And that ❧ *4. "And I shall not worship that which you are worshipping.* ❧ refers to any future time. As the present tense verb, in the first verse indicated the current time, while the active particle indicates the future time and period. ❧ *2. "I worship not that which you worship,* ❧ meaning now or today ❧ *5. "Nor will you worship that which I worship.* ❧ also meaning today. ❧ *4. "And I shall not worship that which you are worshipping.* ❧ meaning in the future ❧ *5. "Nor will you worship that which I worship* ❧ likewise meaning in the future.

However, reflecting on this explanation, how could we accurately say that *(5. **Nor will you worship that which I worship**.)* applied to those Arabs in that age in light of the fact that many of them eventually came to believe and then worshipped Allaah? Due to this important point this offered explanation also has some weakness. Yet those who offer this explanation respond saying that those Allaah whom intends in his statement *5. "**Nor will you worship that which I worship**"* are only those people Allaah, the Most High, knew, would not come to believe. So according to this explanation the address is not general, but specific. Yet there are also additional factors which also indicate the general weakness of this particular explanation. As such, we have discussed two possible explanations, the first being that what was meant was emphasis, the second that its meaning refers to them, those Arabs, not ever worshiping in the future.

The third possible explanation of the verse *2. "**I worship not that which you worship**",* is that it means I do not worshipping any of the idols which you worship *5. "**Nor will you worship that which I worship**"* and you do not truly worship Allaah. Similarly the related verse *4. "**And I shall not worship that which you are worshipping. 5. "Nor will you worship that which I worship**.* means in what each considers as worship. By this meaning, my worship is not like your worship, and your worship is not like my worship. This is a negation of the action that is being done and not the actor himself. Meaning it does not negate that false objects are worshiped by people but negates the value and validity of that worship which is being directed wrongly towards them. As such, it is conveying the meaning that the true value and validity of my worship is not like that incorrect worship which you offer.

Moreover, that worship which you are offering is not liked nor valued as the worship I am offering is. Because my worship is being offered purely for the sake of Allaah, whereas your false forms of worship, involve associating other along with Allaah in worship due to Him alone.

The fourth possible explanation, which is the explanation preferred by Sheikh al-Islaam Ibn Taymeeyah, may Allaah have mercy upon him, was that Allaah's statement: ﴾ *2. "I worship not that which you worship*, 5. *"Nor will you worship that which I worship.* ﴿ is pertaining to the nature of the act itself, so it agrees with the first explanation restrictedly in this particular aspect. Whereas the second two verses ﴾ *4. "And I shall not worship that which you are worshipping." *5. "Nor will you worship that which I worship.* ﴿ pertains to the acceptance of that worship done by the parties.

Meaning that I, the Muslim, will never accept that there is any form of true worship other than what I am offering to Allaah, and similarly you will not accept that there is any way of accepted worship other than what you are performing through wrongly associating others with Allaah. So the first statement of two verses, pertains to the action of worship, whereas the second statement contained in the next two verses, pertains to the acceptance and being pleased with the other contrasted way of worshipping, by those engaging in each of them. Meaning I do not worship those partners which you do along with Allaah, and it is not acceptable nor pleasing to me. Likewise, you do not truly worship Allaah alone, refuse to accept this, and are not pleased with my directing of worship to Him alone with no associates in that worship.

This last statement of explanation of these verses, when one examines and considers it, we find that it is not subject to the noted points of criticism which can be made about the other possible explanations. As such is quite an excellent explanation.

From the point of this conclusion, we can assert generally that there is no instance of repetition of verses in the Qur'aan where there is not benefit found in that repetition. There are no examples of repetition except that there is some benefit in understanding and explaining which can be taken from that repetition. Since if someone were to wrong claim that there are instances of repetition in the Qur'aan without any distinct benefit, then the Qur'aan would fall into possibly being described as containing some aspects of speech without actual value. But it is far exalted above this even to the slightest degree.

Therefor based upon this, the repetition of verses which is found in Surah ar-Rahman ❧ ***Then which of the Blessings of your Lord will you both (jinn and men) deny?*** ❧ as well as that found in Surah al-Mursalaat with the verse: ❧ ***10. Woe, that Day, to those who deny*** ❧ actually conveys to us benefits in understanding which are tremendous. In the first example, that benefit is found with every verse, between these verses which repeat themselves, each of them is specifically a tremendous blessing. Additionally, we understand from this that these blessings are significant favors from Allaah. Furthermore it also contains a benefit in term of its phrasing, by offering a continuous warning to those it is addressing through the repeated verse ❧ ***Then which of the Blessings of your Lord will you both (jinn and men) deny?*** ❧ as well as the repetition of the verse ❧ ***Woe, that Day, to those who deny (Allaah, His Angels, His Books, His Messengers, the Day of Resurrection, and Al-Qadr (Divine Preordainment)*** ❧.

Lastly in this specific surah, Allah, the Most Glorified and the Most Exalted, says ❴ *6. "To you be your religion, and to me my religion"* ❵. ❴ *To you be your religion* ❵ meaning that path which you are upon and the way worship is directed within your life.

❴ *...and to me my religion* ❵ meaning I am free and separated from your way and religion, just as you are separated and have no connection my way and religion of Islaam."

(2)

EMBRACE ISLAAM COMPLETELY & FULLY NOT PARTIALLY

In our daily lives as Muslims, just as found in the words of our noble scholars who work continually to guide the Muslim Ummah, there are many different methodologies and perspectives seen among the Muslims today. There are many conflicting understanding and ways both among those callers and speakers striving to call to our religion and improve the weak situation of the Muslim Ummah as well as among those general Muslims simply striving to realize the guidance of Islaam in their daily lives. However there is an essential question, that our scholars like Sheikh al-Albaanee, may Allaah have mercy upon him, when discussing the present situation of the Muslims and how to improve it,[1]

> *"The Prophet, may Allaah's praise and salutations be upon him, said that {...**if you do such and such wrongdoing Allaah will place a humiliation upon you until you turn back to your religion.**}[2] Therefore it is established that it is required that we, as an Ummah, return back to our religion of Islaam- as the cure to our weak condition.*
>
> *But to which understanding of Islaam do we return to? Is it Islaam as it is understood by these later generations or as it was understood by the first generations? This is the issue that we must enter into to clarify. Is it according to the understanding of the sect of the Mu'tazilah, or the sect of the Matureedeeyah? Or the sect of the 'Ash'arees, or the Shee'ah, or the Raafidhah? As these ways are all present today..."*

---

[1] Questions Regarding the Call to the Way of the First generations: Question No. 3
[2] Authentic narration: Sunan Abu Dawud: no. 3462

The majority of the many calls and offered solutions heard among Muslim today have deficiencies and flaws due to not being fully based, or truly confirming to the guidance of the Messenger of Allaah and his clear methodology, may the praise and salutations of Allaah be upon him and his household. This was found in lesson 3 in the discussed by Sheikh Muhammd 'Amaan al-Jaamee. It is for this very reason our scholars have continually warned against, blindly accepting and supporting these calls without weighing and examining how correct they are, when weighed directly on scales of the Prophet's exemplary life and revealed methodology of calling to and realizing the guidance of Islaam. Sheikh Ahmad an-Najmee, may Allaah have mercy upon him, warned young committed Muslims against neglecting this saying[3], "

> *"So I say: May Allaah have mercy upon the author, as he has guided the people to benefit with this statement, and commanded that one act cautiously and with deliberation when entering into newly developed or arisen affairs in the religion. If you hear someone inviting and calling to the methodology of the group known as the "Muslim Brotherhood", then do not be hasty in accepting it, and do not simply accept his praise of this methodology. If you hear someone calling to the methodologies of the followers of Muhammad Suroor, or the followers of Sayyed Qutb, or the group known as 'Jama'at at-Tableegh', then do not be hasty in accepting their methodologies and entering yourself into adopting these ways until you ask, investigate, and research.*
>
> *You should consider carefully and research either with someone who has an understanding of that methodology but who has not actually embraced it, or from one who previously accepted that way and then turned away it,*

---

[3] From 'The Distinct Guidance in Explaining the Book, 'Explanation of the Sunnah' by al-Imaam al-Barberhaaree': Pages 35-36

or with one who has read sufficiently about them so that they can clarify to you the reality of that group. For if you act hastily, you will find yourself in a difficult situation and within the web of group affiliation and partisanship which only wants to take possession of you by entering you into their ranks or organization. After this, you would then stand as one who innovates in the religion and as one who defends those who innovate in the religion. So I say: from Allaah we come and to Him shall we return! How many have been sacrificed to these methodologies by hastily entering into them, how many have been victimized within their dangerous trap before they actually understood their errors and deficiencies!!

Certainly this is what occurs to individuals in these organizations and groups. Due to this I clearly warn you, just as the author of this text, meaning the author of the book Sharh as-Sunnah, has warned you. I warn you against hastily entering these groups and parties, and I call you to act carefully, cautiously, and to investigate beforehand. Take and read from the books authored in criticism of these groups and parties. Take from such works, meaning these investigative works, and read about these groups and parties before you enter into any of them. And if you find the truth in these works, then do not give preference to anything above it."

Sheikh Saaleh Ibn Sa'd as-Suhaymee explained that one of the fundamental deficiencies of these various modern groups and movements is that their severely unbalanced understanding, has lead to the adoption of false priorities and a distorted practice of the guidance of Islaam. He, may Allaah preserve him, explained how the way proceeded upon by the first generations differed from these modern ways by truly, fully and practically embracing the entire religion, giving every matter its proper place and priority, in his statement,[4]

> *"The eighth foundation: To adopt and embrace all of Islaam, giving true importance to every matter connected to the guidance of the religion without exception. As the correct methodology for one who believes in Islaam is to not be lax or negligent of any single matter, large or small, connected to his religion. Such that whenever a matter reaches him from the Book of Allaah, or from the Sunnah of the Messenger of Allaah, may Allaah's praise and salutations of Allaah be upon him, he does not move in any way except to stand and say "We hear and we obey."As Allaah says,* **The only saying of the faithful believers, when they are called to Allaah (His Words, the Qur'aan) and His Messenger, to judge between them, is that they say: "We hear and we obey." And such are the prosperous ones (who will live forever in Paradise).** *-(Surah An-Nur: 51)*
>
> *And Allaah says,* **It is not for a believer, man or woman, when Allaah and His Messenger have decreed a matter that they should have any option in their decision. And whoever disobeys Allaah and His Messenger, he has indeed strayed in a plain error.** *-(Surah Al-Ahzaab: 36)*
>
> *And Allaah says,* **O you who believe! Answer Allaah (by obeying Him) and (His) Messenger when he () calls you to that which will give you life, and know that Allaah comes in between a person and his heart (i.e. He prevents an evil person to decide anything). And verily to Him you shall (all) be gathered.** *-(Surah Al-Anfal: 24)*
>
> *One should not take hold of one aspect of Islaam's guidance but turn away and abandon other aspects of Islaam. Because there are some Muslims wrongly following*

---

[4] Taken from 'The Foundations Upon Which The Methodology of Following the First Generations is Based'

different modern devised innovated methodologies, that generally focus on limited or particular aspects of the guidance of our religion. They falsely believe that their biased restricted viewpoint is sufficient for everyone to adopt and implement, and that others, as Muslims, should abandon any and every other way and priority than their developed way. Examples of this are those Muslims who continually speak and focus on political power, and gaining positions of societal control, as well those focused upon current events, broadcast news, and those sources and commentators of it from modern media outlets. They simply squander away most of their time upon this limited focus and aspect.

Another group of Muslims focuses on those aspects which they wrongly supposed reflects a correct abstinence from the world and a true devotion to worship, whereas in reality it is an modern expression of misguided Sufism which has been imposed upon us and brought into our land of the two holy cities from outside this land. They implement this perspective, by going out and travelling through the earth calling, and this is considered the most significant endeavor within Islaam in their view!

Another group of Muslims, have actually abandoned and rejected some of the core fundamentals of Islaam, for the sake of pleasing nations or other peoples who are Christians and Jews. Yet Allaah informs us, ❧**Never will the Jews nor the Christians be pleased with you (O Muhammad Peace be upon him) till you follow their religion. Say: "Verily, the Guidance of Allaah (i.e. Islamic Monotheism) that is the (only) Guidance. And if you (O Muhammad Peace be upon him) were to follow their (Jews and Christians) desires after what you have received of Knowledge (i.e. the Qur'aan), then you would have against Allaah neither any walee (protector or guardian) nor any helper.** ❧*-(Surah Al-Baqarah: 12)*

Another group of Muslims have adopted the perspective that [the ends justifies the means] in their various efforts. Such that if the goal is legitimate then they struggle to achieve it by any possible means or available method necessary even if by one which clearly prohibited in the guidance of Islaam! For example, they proceed to engage in calling to Allaah with different methods which have been imported from other cultures and lands, such as using fictional dramas, theatrical plays, and audio nasheeds. They use such methods which are effective in attracting and gathering multitudes of all kinds of people, since their first focus is simply gathering everyone together who says they are Muslims. They claim to do this for Islaam but this is done without considering the actual beliefs of those various individuals whom they have gathered together! They do this, under the banner of, and implementing the false derived principle of [We gather together upon whatever joins us together, and we excuse each others in the many things that we differ with each other about.]

Yet another group from among those seen as Muslims have come to actually reject and completely turn away from the religion altogether. Because they have come to see it as something strange and unusual, so they have undone the bonds connecting them to Islaam and become westernized in their beliefs and their manners and are very distant our religion generally. They view it, meaning the religion of Islaam, as something which is not suitable nor a way able to bring about success and well being. Furthermore, they hold that it is intolerant and outdated.

In respect to each and every one of these groups, it is an obligation for you as a Muslim, to stay away from and declare yourself free from them and their misguidance, and to strive to proceed upon the original path of the truth. This is accomplished by your taking our religion, each and every part of it, from its original sources, taking it in relation to our beliefs, our understanding of ritual acts of worship, our general rulings and guidance of the religion, our character as individuals, our manners, as well as in our protecting Muslim societies through implementing deterring criminal punishments in Islaam, meaning in every single aspects and area of our lives.

Sheikh Bakr Abu Zayd, may Allaah have mercy upon him, explained what distinguishes that straight path of the first Muslims when compared to various incorrect methodologies found today among Muslims of different modern movements and groups. He, may Allaah have mercy upon him, explained how their false perspectives hurt a Muslim in terms of knowledge as well as practice. He said,[5]

"Be a Salafee who proceeds upon that clear path, investigating the reports of transmitted knowledge from the early centuries, following the established evidenced ways of guidance, as someone calling to Allaah upon knowledge and insight, someone who recognizes the merit of the people of distinctive merit, and who strives to compete with them in attaining good.

Certainly, blameworthy partisanship which is present, with it's newly devised structures and methods that the early Muslims had no knowledge of, is from the most significant barriers to the Muslims gaining Sharee'ah knowledge, and splitting the united body of Muslims. Indeed, how many different ways has this misguided partisanship weakened the rope of Muslim unity, and deceived the Muslims through it's various deceptions?

---

[5] Hilyah Taalib al-Ilm pg.61

As such, be warned, may Allaah have mercy upon you, from these groups and parties, and be warned away from simply choosing to go around spending your days circulating around their invented focuses and devised ways, and eventually suffering the consequences of the evil which results from what they practice. As the reality of their way is to handle the various types people like one sees with a gutter and downspout from a roof, first it gathers together all kinds of individuals like mixed muddy waters and then eventually only splashing them around uselessly with little effect or true change. Today, this occurs generally among many, except for with those people whom your Lord in His mercy protects from that affliction, and guides them to stand upon the same guidance which the Prophet and his Companions previously stood upon, may Allaah be pleased with all of them.

Moreover all of this is intrinsically done while conforming to the needs of constantly changing situations and circumstances, since the guidelines of Islaam account for this, and properly put every matter of life in its rightful place. This is especially true in relation to those individuals involved in the efforts of calling people to Islaam, and those callers engaged in this area. It is only proper and quite necessary that such callers recognize and understand the true situation of weakness, and the fundamental aliment present among Muslims. As without question, the Muslims today need discussions and explanations of the correct beliefs.

The Muslims also need discussions and explanations about the place of balanced abstention from worldly matters, piety, and focusing on ritual worship. They also need discussions and explanations about developing upright excellent character. They also need discussions and explanations about fighting and combating against the commission of sins and wrongdoing, all of these undertaken through the well known acknowledged legitimate ways of doings so found with the Sharee'ah.

This is since the religion of Islaam is a single sound methodology, not merely isolated parts or aspects. Indeed, Allaah has said, ❦ ***And verily! This your religion (of Islamic Monotheism) is one religion, and I am your Lord, so keep your duty to Me.*** ❦ *-(Surah Al-Mu'minun: 52)*

Similarly, further building upon this and clarifying the mistake of those who try to falsely present that there are different types or versions of following the first generations, Sheikh Muhammad Baazmool, mentions,

"Salafeeyah, or the way of the Salaf, means to proceed upon the path which the Messenger of Allaah, may the praise and salutations of Allaah be upon him, and his Companions proceeded upon. It is, in its reality that methodology of the life which every Muslim should proceed upon, as Allaah says ❦ ***He has no partner. And of this I have been commanded, and I am the first of the Muslims.*** ❦ *-(Surah Al-An'am: 163)*

As such, we do not restrict the way of the Salaf to seeking knowledge, so it is not correct to say [knowledge focused Salafeeyah]

Nor do we restrict the way of the Salaf to militarily striving in the path of Allaah, so it is not correct to say [Jihad focused Salafeeyah]

Nor should we say [blind following focused Salafeeyah]. Because Salafeeyah, or the way of the Salaf, means preceding upon what ever the Prophet and his Companions proceeded upon, so then how could we say about undertaking this that it was [blind following

focused Salafeeyah]!?

Nor should we attach or connect Salafeeyah, to something other than proceeding as a Muslim upon what the righteous Salaf proceeded upon, in their adherence and following of the Messenger of Allaah. So Salafeeyah cannot be [the Salafeeyah of so-and-so from the scholars] or [Salafeeyah from so-and-so from among the callers]! Rather Salafeeyah is purer Islaam taking from those original sources which are truly sufficient for this Ummah.

This is for anyone who wants to stand upon that which the Messenger of Allaah, and his Companions stood upon, as they are the Jamaa'ah.

Those who are upon Salafeeyah, only declare as disbelievers those individuals for whom the evidenced ruling of Allaah, the Most High, and his Messenger, may the praise and salutations of Allaah be upon him, clearly indicates their disbelief.

Additionally those upon Salafeeyah, struggle in the path of Allaah against those whom Allaah, the Most High, and his Messenger, may the praise and salutations of Allaah be upon him, have clearly indicated we should strive against them.

Likewise, those upon Salafeeyah, have allegiance and allies themselves with those whom Allaah, the Most High, and his Messenger, may the praise and salutations of Allaah be upon him, have clearly indicated we should have allegiance with them. The one who was outside of affirming and implementing these matters, stand outside the boundaries of Salafeeyah.

For that reason the one who declares someone as a disbeliever, and about that individual the evidences do not show that Allaah and His Messenger, may the praise and salutations of Allaah be upon him, in their meaning declare them to be upon disbelief, then the one who wrongly declared thus has opposed the way of the Salaf.

And the one who fights against anyone, whom Allaah and His Messenger, may the praise and salutations of Allaah be upon him, have not commanded the Muslims to fight against him, then the one who doing so has opposed the way of the Salaf.

And the one who has allegiance and allies themselves to anyone, whom Allaah and His Messenger, may the praise and salutations of Allaah be upon him have not commanded the Muslims have allegiance and ally themselves with, then he has opposed the way of the Salaf.

So how can anyone truthfully attributes to the way of the Salaf, those individuals who stand outside its way, and proceed as those who oppose its path?!"

We ask Allaah to guide us to every matter of belief and deeds which is pleasing to Him from His completed perfected religion. And we ask Him alone to lead every Muslim man and woman towards what will increase His love of us, and to distance and turn us away from every matters displeasing to Him, which leads to His anger falling upon us.

(3)

THE REMEMBRANCE OF ALLAAH & MERITS OF GATHERINGS OF DHIKR

Various Scholars

The people who love the Sunnah, those struggling everyday to walk in the footsteps of the first generations of Muslims and those in every century who adhered to their 'believers way', hold that dhikr or remembrance, is an important means to be successful in both this world and the next. It is authentically narrated that the Messenger of Allaah, may Allaah's praise and salutations be upon him, said,

{There will not anything at all that a person can do that is more effective in saving him from the punishment of Allaah that engaging in the remembrance of Allaah.} [1]

This belief has been held by the leading scholars in every century, as they are indeed the inheritors of the Messenger of Allaah. The tremendous scholar of numerous Islamic sciences, Ibn al-Qayyim, may Allaah have mercy upon him, stated,[2]

"There is nothing that illuminates both the hearts and the graves of those who engaged in it, which is equivalent to the remembrance of Allaah."

Ibn al-Jawzee, may Allaah have mercy upon him, correspondingly reminded us of the sever danger in neglecting it,[3]

"Nothing is more harmful to a worshiper of Allaah than two things: his being heedless of the remembrance of Allaah, and his failing to submit suitably to the commands of Allaah."

---

[1] Narrated in the Musnad of Imaam Ahmad: 22079, and authenticated by Sheikh al-Albaanee in his verification of Saheeh al-Jaamea': narration number 5733
[2] al-Waabil as-Sayyib: pg. 50
[3] at-Tadhkiraah fee Wa'ath: pg 102

For this reason, we should each ask ourselves, firstly how and what do we understand what is dhikr or the remembrance of Allaah as reflected in the authentic Sunnah? Secondly, how should it be implemented and how can we truly make it something, as mentioned, that acts as a shield and keeps us from falling into Allaah's punishment for our negligence as His worshippers? What role does dhikr have in our efforts to always turn back towards and return to Allaah when we regularly fall short as worshippers affected by many influences that surround us everyday? This is something which needs to be clarified for every sincere Muslim working for Allaah's pleasure For this reason Ibn Taymeeyah, may Allah have mercy upon him reminded us that,[4]

> *"That worldly trial or tribulation which leads you to turn back and become closer to Allaah, is of greater benefit to you, than what is generally seen as a blessing but which actually leads you to slip into forgetting the remembrance of Allaah, the Most Glorified and the Most Exalted."*

Sheikh Muhammad Ibn 'Umar Baazmool discussed the importance of our returning back to Allaah, and the role of remembrance within that from the evidenced guidance of Islaam. He, may Allaah preserve him, mentioned that,[5]

> *"... ❧ So flee Allaah (from His Torment to His Mercy ❧. The meaning of this is that there is no doubt that for each of us, there those who want evil and what bad to reach and afflict you, there are several opponents all around you watching for opportunity to harm you, as well as there being many things in this world that can divert you away from the truth. You are, as a Muslim, certainly surrounded by those who oppose you, such that you want to escape and find refuge from all of that. And Allaah says,*

---
[4] Jaame' al-Masa'il, vol. 9, pg. 387
[5] Taken from the Facebook page of Sheikh Muhammad Baazmool

❃No! There is no refuge! Unto your Lord (Alone) will be the place of rest that Day. ❃-(Surah Al-Qiyaamah: 11-12). Yet this clearly applies to an event connected to the next life. So how are can we find refuge and safety from these matters that confront us in this world? It is upon you to turn and engage in the remembrance of Allaah, and turn towards the seeking of Sharee'ah knowledge. This is your true way to flee to Allaah and seek refuge in Him in this world.

*It is through the engagement in remembering Allaah that one's heart comes to have peace and to be at ease. The Messenger of Allaah said, {"**The singular individuals are unequaled and have excelled.**" He was asked, 'Who are those individuals who are unequaled?' He replied, "**Those men and women who frequently focus and engage in the remembrance of Allaah.**"} (Saheeh Muslim: 1436)[6] Similarly, those who proceed upon a path of seeking beneficial knowledge, as they are those for whom Allaah makes easy the path to entering Jannah."*

This narration about those who have excelled, like the earlier narration, reminds us of the tremendous benefit and importance of 'dhikr' or remembrance which is something accepted by all Muslims. Yet the issue of what is considered acceptable dhikr or what actually falls within the meaning of true remembrance is one where there are many different claims. Among many Muslims, the source of disagreement in this subject is caused by blindly following a cultural understanding of Islaam found in a specific Muslim countries. As many Muslims generally follow whatever is commonly asserted to be acceptable expressions, practices, and methods of ritual <u>remembrance,</u> used to rectify and purify our souls, found

---

[6] Sheikh al-'Utheimen in his explanation of Riyadh as-Saaliheen explains this expression in the hadeeth saying "...They are those who are surpass others because they work, focus, and struggle more than others upon goodness. Such that they outstrip and excel others in the obtaining of that which is good. And the success is from Allaah alone."

with the people of that land where they are from or live. Often what Muslims consider beneficial common practices of dhikr used to rectify and purify our souls, are accepted regardless of whether or not that practice was something actually taught by the Messenger of Allaah, may the praise and salutations of Allaah be upon him, or not. The danger in this is the taking a path, claimed to lead to rectification and success, without sure knowledge that it is what our beloved Prophet actually proceeded upon. We are not able to recognize where we fall short as Muslims, unless both we have the right criterion and correct way to do so. About this important self-examination for Ibn al-Qayyim, may Allaah have mercy upon him, stated,[7]

> *"Within the efforts of an individual to call themselves to account for what they do in their life, there are a number of aspects connected to self-rectification. Among them is becoming aware and considering your shortcomings, as the one who does not become aware of their mistakes and faults is not able to work towards rectifying and removing them."*

From our mistakes and faults as submissive worshippers can be a personal failure to ask, "Is what I am doing what our Messenger diad and taught his Companions to do?" In striving to truly follow the Sunnah we should each strive to weigh where we stand in terms of the light of the tremendous blessing in the example of some successfully engaged in dhikr, or remembrance which we have in the life model of the Messenger of Allaah, may the praise and salutations of Allaah be upon him, and his family.

Often Muslims do not weigh and evaluate the support or lack of it in the revealed source texts for these various beliefs, practices, or methodologies common in their land which are connected to 'dhikr' because they do not realize that they practices were developed long after the age of the

---

[7] Aid for the Yearning One in Resisting the Attacks of Shaytaan: vol. 1 pg. 84

Prophet and his noble upright Companions, may Allaah be pleased with them all. This negligence to connect ourselves to the first and best example of remembrance of Allaah is unfortunately similar to the practice of modern day Christianity where the vast majority of claims by modern day Christians made about the details of their practices, including dhikr, have no direct connection to the beliefs that the Prophet 'Isa originally conveyed and taught to those submissive supporting worshippers who accepted his message, and originally held that correct belief in their hearts and lives.

Additionally, similar to what is commonly seen among Christians, there is also confusion caused by many Muslims adopting superficial practices that are regarded as sufficient reflections of dhikr that they assume Allaah will be pleased with, wrongly believing these fulfill the need for dhikr in their lives. Yet the senior scholars upon the true Sunnah in the modern age, such Sheikh Saaleh Fauzaan al-Fauzaan, may Allaah preserve him, have opposed that understanding, distinguishing what is actually the dhikr Allaah desires from us.[8]

> *"The remembrance of Allaah is not simply changing the ringtone of your phone to something presumed Islamic, rather remembrance is the recitation of the Qur'aan, efforts related to narrating hadeeth, sound statements of remembrance such as Allaahu akbar, and such as the calling of the adhaan.*
>
> *It is not simply changing the ringtone of your phone, or selecting something considered "Islamic" as alerts for your conversations with others. As these matters contain what something which is an insult and mockery to actual remembrance of Allaah, the Most Glorified and the Most Exalted."*

---

[8] Statements of Guidance for The Muslim Soldiers #23

We must ask ourselves do we personally understand and practice dhikr correctly? Sheikh al-'Utheimeen, may Allaah have mercy upon him, was asked, "**What is intended by the term 'remembrance of Allaah? Does this mean only the recitation of the Qur'aan or only sending prayers and good mention upon our Prophet, may Allaah's praise and salutations be upon him, or does it refer to all the statements of remembrance transmitted to us?**"[9]

"Answer: The remembrance of Allaah generally encompasses every matter or endeavor that draws and brings a person closer to Allaah, the Most Glorified and the Most Exalted, regardless of whether that be with one's heart, or one's tongue, or with the limbs of ones body.

As for the specific meaning, such as what is found in the statement of Allaah, ❧**When you have finished as-Salaat (the prayer - congregational), remember Allaah standing, sitting down, and lying down on your sides,...**❧-*(Surah An-Nisa': 103) Then what this intends what is found within the Sunnah from the well know statements of dhikr such as saying "La illaha illaa Allaah", saying "Allaahu akbar", saying "SubhanAllaah", saying "Astaghfirullah", and those supplication that mention praise of Allaah the Most Perfect and the Most High, such as, "Oh Allaah you are as-Salaam, and from you comes peace, how blessed are You oh possessor of Majesty and Nobility."*

But it is important to understand that, the general remembrance by which Allaah praises His worshippers for is much broader and comprehensive than the specific forms of stated remembrance. This is since remembrance can be engaged in with the heart, it can be engaged in with the tongue, and it can be performs by the limbs of the body.

---

[9] Taken from the website for the Sheikh http://binothaimeen.net- Audio file #102_08

That remembrance which may be engaged in with the heart, is for example, thinking about and considering the various signs of Allaah within His path and revealed system of guidance as well as the numerous signs found around us in creation. Similarly an example of it is inwardly trusting in Allaah, desiring closeness to Him, fully loving and depending on him, and those inwards acts which are similar to these.

That remembrance which may be engaged in with the tongue, is very clear, every statement which draws someone close to Allaah the Most High from those specific evidenced statements of remembrance, the reading and recitation of the Qur'aan, verbally enjoining what is good and preventing wrongdoing, and teaching beneficial knowledge to others.

That remembrance which may be engaged in with the body is, every endeavor or act which brings someone closer to Allaah the Most High, such as the ritual prayer with it positions of standing, sitting, bowing, and prostrating to Allaah alone, the earning of livelihood for dependant, the giving of charity to those deserving of it, and acting similar to these in nature.

For this reason, it is essential and needed that one understands the difference between the broader general meaning of remembrance in Islaam, and the specific detailed meaning of remembrance."

Sheikh Muhammad Ibn Saaleh al-'Utheimeen, may Allaah have mercy upon him, also stressed the importance of understanding this and not neglecting this focus which the Messenger of Allaah, may the praise and salutations of Allaah be upon him, reflected in every aspect of his life.

This understanding held by him, Sheikh al-'Utheimeen, which was taken from the source texts and the understanding of them which the first generations of the Ummah held, directly and explicitly opposes the incorrect restricted understanding of dhikr many of the people of innovation have focused upon which has distorted its true comprehensive meaning. [10]

> *"Have taqwa of Allaah, oh worshippers, and frequently seek to gain the tremendous rewards available from those actions and endeavors which are easy. Frequently engage in the remembrance of Allaah, the Most Glorified and the Most Exalted, with your hearts, and your tongues, as well as your bodies. Such that remembrance of Allaah, the Most High become established clearly within your hearts whether you are standing, sitting, or relaxing on your sides.*
>
> *Be those who continually pursue remembering the tremendous majesty of Allaah and His transcendence. Be those who remember Him through the careful consideration of His perfect names, attributes, and actions. As in every matter coming from Him there are indeed signs in that creation that remind you of Him, of His majesty, and which lead you to contemplate His essential nature of being unique with nothing similar to Him. These matters remind you of His power, His incredible grandeur, and which reflect the effects of His incredible mercy and wisdom in creation.*
>
> *Remember Allaah the Most High with your tongues, by making the affirmed statements of dhikr "La ilaha ilaa Allaah" "SubhanAllaah", "Alhamdulillah", and "Allaahu akbar." Know that engaging in and making every statement of established goodness by which you are seeking the face of Allaah, is certainly counted as being*

---

[10]

from the remembrance of Allaah. Likewise, remember Allaah the Most High with your bodies by engaging in acts of worship and obedience, and distancing yourself from acts of sin and transgression. Since every action whether moving towards and engaging in the first, or turning away and leaving the second, by which the overall obedience of Allaah and gaining closeness to him is actually realized, is considered a form of dhikr of Allaah in the Sharee'ah.

Therefore, engage yourself in making significant remembrance of Allaah, the Most High, do not be someone whom Allaah allows their heart to be turned away from His remembrance, slipping into being a person who generally follows their unchecked desires, and so becoming someone who is lost and life is simply wasted. Rather engage in significant remembrance of Allaah, before some impediment comes between you and your remembrance of Him, whether that be through actually dying, losing your capabilities due to old age, or even before you may be deprived and lose many of the blessing you have as a punishment for your being heedless of His proper remembrance.

Oh Muslim, do not allow yourself to be someone preoccupied away from the remembrance of Allaah by the pursuit of worldly wealth or by only focusing on your families and children. As the passing enjoyment of our families and children are the adornment of the life of this world, where as the righteous endeavors that we engage in and more important and significant, in terms of what we should hope for benefit from, and seek His rewards for. That which is of greatest value to your Lord are those righteous deeds which remain that are not lost upon our death, every form of righteous actions. Undoubtedly, from the most significant of them are those valid statements of dhikr such as "SubhanAllaah", "Alhamdulillah", "La ilaha ilaa Allaah", "Allaahu akbar", and "La hawla wa la Quwaata Ilaa Billah." Oh worshippers of Allaah the Most High, the remembrance of Allaah is something which an easy profit to make and a simple yield to harvest. it is that which if you are heedless of doing it, you will only find yourself damaged and in a true state of loss."

This shows that our beloved sheikh believes what every scholar upon the Sunnah adhered to. As Ibn Qayyim, may Allaah have mercy upon him, stated,[11]

"From the signs of a healthy heart is that it rarely ceases remembering Allaah, it never truly gets tired of serving Him, and it never gets accustomed to being attached to other than Him, except those close to Him whom He directs it towards. It remembers Him, and is engaged in thinking about Him inwardly".

Similarly Sheikh 'Abdul-'Azeez ar-Raajhee, may Allaah preserve him, gives us insight on how pursuing those sitting of remembrance that focus upon authentic non-innovative knowledge brings the worshipper many significant benefits in their lives. He also has explained clearly the comprehensive nature of general dhikr or remembrance, according to the people following the path of the Prophets clear established Sunnah, and here specifically indicated the numerous benefits of such gatherings of authentic knowledge, mentioning,[12]

"...As for the various satisfactions and delights from among the different merits of sittings of remembrance: from the most significant of them related to gaining understanding and which are greatest in goodness are: knowledge of the names and attributes of Allaah the Most High, His affirmed actions, and comprehending

---

[11] Aid for the Yearning One in Resisting the Attacks of Shaytaan: pg. 72
[12] A Treatise on Cultivation Upon Islaam: pgs. 66-67

His sublime worthiness of being worshipped alone.

From them is gaining knowledge of what is permissible and impermissible, what matters bring benefit and which cause harm.

From them is gaining knowledge of the guidelines what some might specifically engage within the affairs of buying and selling, renting, share-cropping and agricultural agreements, as well as understanding how to justly interact with people daily.

From their benefit them is gaining knowledge of the rights of your parents, the rights of your wives and children, those of your close relatives, as well as the rights of your neighbors, the poor, and widows.

Generally from them a person is able to learn how to worship His Lord fully upon insight and understanding of his religion.

You come to understand the knowledge of excellent character which can raise an individual up to the highest of positions and levels, alongside knowledge of what good manners to practice.

From them is gaining knowledge of how to personify and realize good within oneself, striving removing what is evil, controlling both ones desires and ones fears, directing the soul towards undertaking different forms of goodness and abandoning different forms of wrongdoing, while attaching it to the various affairs of life which bring it benefit.

From them is gaining knowledge of of the noble Arabic language along with its various advantages, the uses of its different areas of study, the benefits which this brings to one's language skills, and how it guides the clarity in your expressions.

From them is gaining knowledge of the various periods and ages of history, previous empires, the different categories and types of nations and civilizations, as well as contemporary modern reflections of earlier nations and people.

Therefore by being in beneficial sittings of remembrance an individual is continually guided towards having a clear criterion by which to distinguish between truth and falsehood, towards recognizing the one who has been enticed into misguidance from the one who has remained upon the truth, as well as towards understanding what are actually beneficial endeavors and which ways in fact only lead us towards harm and negative consequences."

Ibn Taymeeyah, may Allaah have mercy upon him,[13]

"It is a necessity that worshiper of Allaah have time when he dedicates himself to supplicating, engaging in ritual remembrance, performing ritual prayers, contemplating matters, calling himself to account, struggling to rectify his heart, that those endeavors which are specifically connected to these matters."

Sheikh Muhammad Ibn Saaleh al-'Utheimeen, may Allaah the Most High have mercy upon him, said,[14]

"I advise my Muslim brothers to be diligent in implementing those practices of the Sunnah which are affirmed from the Messenger of Allaah , may Allaah's praise and salutation be upon him and his family, and to turn away from that which is not affirmed as coming from him.

---

[13] Majmu'a al-Fataawa: vol. 10 pg. 426
[14] Fatawaa Fel-'Aqeedah: vol. 2 page 1129

As the Messenger of Allaah, may Allaah's praise and salutation be upon him and his family, did not leave any single matter which the Muslim Ummah needed for its success in this world or its success in the next world to come, except that he explained it and made it clear."

This echoes that general advice which the Companions gave to the next generation coming after them to embrace everything that was part of the truth of Islaam, including a correct understanding of dhikr. This is found in the narration of 'Uthmaan Ibn Haadher Al-Azdee who said,[15]

"I said to 'Abdullah Ibn 'Abbaas, may Allaah be pleased with him, 'Advise me.'" He replied, "Hold to being steadfast upon the truth, follow that which is guidance, and do not innovate new matters."

From this is their understanding what has always been from the revealed guidance leading to Allaah is which is reported from the noble Companion 'Abdullah Ibn Ma'sood, may Allah be pleased with him,[16]

"There was not any prophet from Allaah's many prophets except that when troubled and distressed he turned to verbally saying subhanAllaah, meaning declaring Allaah transcendence above and freedom from any defect or shortcoming, such that they frequently repeatedly this both their times of difficulty as well as in their times of ease."

This shows that not only our Salaf, but the Prophets and messengers before them, generally held that our well being in this world is tied to our engagement in legislated acts of dhikr within our lives.

---

[15] Authentic transmission, Sunan Ad-Daramee vol. 1, page 53, Ibn Wadhaah "Bida'ah wa al-Nahee anhu" pg. 32,
[16] al-Jawaad al-Kaafee of Ibn al-Qayyim, vol.1 pg. 7

Similarly, I close with the reminder, firstly to myself, of the importance of our rewards as striving worshipers of Allaah, which are found in the Hereafter, are also connected and tied to dhikr or the remembrance of our Most Merciful Lord in this world, the place of work and struggle. Ibn al-Qayyim, may Allaah have mercy upon him said,[17]

> *"Certainly, the homes in Jannah are build through our dhikr. If the one remembering Allaah stops engaging in remembrance, the angels stop their building of those abodes in Paradise."*

And the success in this life and the next is from Allaah alone, sufficient is He as a Guardian and Protector.

---

[17] al-Waabil as-Sayyib, pg. 83

(4)

DO NOT BUILD YOUR ISLAAM UPON YOUR INTELLECT OR EMOTIONS- BUT UPON REVELATION

Sheikh Sheikh Saaleh Aal-Sheikh, may Allaah preserve him[1]

The Sharee'ah only has a single directional source from which it is taken, meaning a single door from which it is received, such that there is no functional difference between the area of correct beliefs and that area of practical deeds in relation to the specific sources they are based upon. Both the area of knowledge and the area of actions, have as their source the Book of Allaah and the Sunnah, meaning what comes from revelation. For this reason the author, may Allaah have mercy upon him, stated,

"Certainly no one is safe in his faith, except for the one who is submissive and yielding to Allaah the Most Glorified and the Most Exalted, and conforming to His Messenger, may Allaah's praise and salutations be upon him, and who refers those matters which are ambiguous to him back to someone with clear knowledge of them."

This is because when dealing with the different issues of the correct beliefs or working in the realm of the correct understanding of how to implement the source texts in ones actions, then it is inevitable that some will have difficulties comprehending the explanations or reasons for some matters and that a certain person might have difficulty understanding the benefit of some matters, yet there is no legitimate place for this uncertainty when related to the issues of faith. There is no correct position other than an individual standing clearly upon full compliance and submission to guidance. Because, it is well known and acknowledged that this religion is only established and based upon clear proofs. As such, it must be noted that the various matters or perspectives that different people engage in are divided into three distinct

---

[1] As stated in his "Explanation of Aqeedah at-Tahaweeyah" tape 11

divisions of evidences:

Firstly, emotional or instinctual matters, and its evidences or arguments are natural feelings and instincts. For example someone feels hunger, feels thirst, experiences fear, or acts with mercy towards someone according to his inborn instincts and natural disposition.

The second type are those matters specifically connected to demonstrable intellectual evidences and proofs, and these are matters which the people approach using their intellectual faculties, such that they compare, assess, and inform others of various matters, and whatever is similar to this related to intellectual matters. This is that area of human knowledge which is aided and served by the acceptable study of logic, in a general way.

The third matter or perspective taken as a proof or evidence is: those proofs and arguments directly related to revealed religion. The proofs or arguments which are accepted within the realm of the religion of Islaam can only be based upon the correct foundation, and that foundation is submission to the revealed sources used to derive guidance in the religion.

Due to this, it is mistake to confusedly mix between using and applying these three different types of arguments. As the fundamental source of the religion is not the human intellect, nor is its main source someone's emotional feelings or instincts. Rather its fundamental source can only be one of these three types of arguments discussed. For this reason it validity not validly discussed from the direction of philosophy nor that of classical logic. This type of proof, meaning the fundamental evidence and proof in this religion, is only that which is based solely upon those acknowledged religious foundations which only come from revealed principles.

Furthermore, regarding the legitimacy of this category of revealed proof as compared to the other two different mentioned types, then there is no Muslim, from the different people who adhere to the many different sects of the Muslim Ummah, that disputes the legitimacy of that proof which comes from the Book of Allaah and which comes from the Sunnah. Every one of them generally affirms that what comes from the Book of Allaah and what comes from the Sunnah of the Messenger of Allaah, may Allaah's praise and salutations be upon him, is a clear proof and evidence. As, these two revealed sources, the Book of Allaah and the Sunnah are unquestionably the truth, and they are considered a fundamental proof and evidence.

However what the different sects and groups differ and dispute about is whether the Book of Allaah and the Sunnah are predominant or are the other types of mentioned evidences dominant over and above them? Does the intellect have superior position over the Book of Allaah and the Sunnah or is the intellect is in fact subservient to them? As well as related disputes directly connected to this essential question. This lack of clarity only manifested itself due to most of the sects incorrectly confusing and mixing between these three different types of arguments which have been mentioned. For that reason, the discussion of these fundamental premises are the issue before you to consider, and the issue we are examining.

The people who incorrectly give precedence to their intellects over revealed guidance mix and confuse between the superiority of these three types of arguments. They wrongly place the arguments born of one's intellect and those from revealed proofs from revealed guidance upon a single equivalent level. In fact, they further wrongly place arguments derived through the intellect as dominant over the clear proofs and evidences of revealed guidance. Because of their claim that it is only through utilizing the intellect that we can understand the Sharee'ah and the authenticity of Sharee'ah guidance. Yet this is not correct as will be shown in the following paragraph.

When it is affirmed and established that the Book of Allaah and the Sunnah are the absolute truth, since their origin is only Allaah, the Most Exalted, the Most High, and because the Sunnah itself is also only a form of revelation, then the fundamental and final reference point when seeking proofs and evidences would definitively be the Book and the Sunnah. Such that the one who stands in doubt about this essential affirmation or has some uncertainties about this, then that individual will not be strong in his comprehension of his religion.

As we have mentioned the arguments which people turn to are of three different types:

- Emotional or instinctual arguments,
- or purely intellectual arguments,
- or evidences and proofs based upon revealed guidance.

Emotional or instinctual arguments or affirmations are not consistent nor universal, as the emotional nature of people differs considerably. Similarly, intellectual arguments are also not something consistent or universal among people. This is despite what is stated by these claimants, meaning those who incorrectly give precedence to intellectual conclusions from the adherents of the sects of the Mu'tazilah and the Ash'arees. They claim: [It is only proper that the intellect be given precedence over the revealed Sharee'ah texts.] But the intellect itself is neither consistent nor universal. As whose intellect is the final reference for everyone?

Additionally, it is possible that the intellect of any single person fully grasps all the various issues and matters related to the human condition? No, simply from the perspective of considering its natural limits. A single person's intellect is not even considered the sole reference by the philosophers, as they themselves recognize that various peoples intellects differ considerably according to the natural differences and circumstances found throughout the world among different people. Additionally, even those who give such an incorrect and precarious position to the intellect differ among themselves regarding the requirements and requisites of how to effectively utilize it. They have broadly agreed, in theory, upon the general affirmation and principle of giving precedence to the intellect above all else. However, whose intellects should be practically referred to as the final reference authority, have they actually agreed upon this, no not at all.

Since this is the case, it is clear that there is only a single category or type of proof which it is correct to say there is agreement among Muslims regarding its authority without any disputes. That is the category of revealed proofs found within the Book and the Sunnah. Therefore if someone encounters a dilemma related to what are the correct belief in a specific issue they must refer back by the way of submitting and conforming to the guidance of the Book of Allaah, the Most Exalted and Most High, and back to His Messenger. As the Book of Allaah and the Sunnah are the true proofs and source of evidence. If you personally do not see the reason for a certain aspect of guidance or ruling, then this does not mean that there is a deficiency in the proofs of revealed guidance, rather it means that there is a deficiency in how you have attempted to examine it, or in your properly understanding those revealed proofs. As the unapparent details of the proofs which are evidence in any specific matter, may simply not be clear to everyone.

Similarly, someone lacking understanding could ask regarding different matters of ritual worship such as the prayers: Why are there five daily ritual prayers and not four? Why is salatul-fajr two raka'ats and not three? Why is Hajj performed in the exact manner it is and not some another way? Why do we purify ourselves in the exact way that we do? The answer is that all of these matters are based upon submission and compliance to revealed guidance, meaning submission and compliance to the Book of Allaah and the Sunnah.

This area of research which Imaam at-Tahawee mentions in this sentence has been named by some of the modern day people of knowledge, with a modern term which means, "the singular absolute source for deriving the religion". Moreover, this issue of affirming the correct sources of deriving where the religion is taken from is from the most important of issues which is required be examined by us. As if you and I differ regarding any matter of Islaam, then it is necessary that there be a single reference as a proof such that we can go to and refer to it.

The people, meaning all of the different sects, in relation to the methods they have adopted for deriving the matters of the Sharee'ah of Islaam, are divided into three different categories:

The first category: those who refer primarily to the intellect, meaning those who place the intellect as that which should judge and determine the validity of the revealed texts of the Sharee'ah, and they make the guidelines of the Sharee'ah that which is subservient to their intellectual conclusions.

The second category: those who consider the Sharee'ah and the derivations of its rulings to be devoid and free from having the intellect hold any place or role to assist in understanding to any degree whatsoever. Rather to them the Sharee'ah is only transmitted knowledge without having any discernible causes or explanation for its matters whether in the area of beliefs or in the realm of practical deeds and endeavors.

The third category: those who stand correctly between these two opposing groups. They hold that in relation to the rulings of the Sharee'ah, in connection to explaining what the Sharee'ah encompasses of transmitted beliefs regarding matters of the unseen worlds, as well as in understanding what are beneficial legislated actions, that the intellect plays a beneficial role. They affirm that the intellect acts as a servant for the Sharee'ah but is never something predominant over it. Such that we should benefit from the intellect through the clarification and understanding of the causes of matters, their rulings, as well as in properly understanding the Sharee'ah and deriving sound principles and concepts from it. Because it is Allaah Himself, who made the Qur'aan as a Book intended for those who consider and reflect upon matters. These three are the major divisions or perspectives of methodology among the people of the Ummah historically.

- The first division includes those like the astray sects of the Jahmeeyah, the Mu'tazilah, as well as the Ashaa'reeyah, restrictedly, in some of their general developed principles of investigation and consideration of affairs.

- The second division includes those like those historically referred to as the Dhaahireeyah among the schools of fiqh, as seen in their incorrect way of deriving the rulings of the religion, and likewise in some of their incorrect positions in matters of belief. It also applies to the Ash'aareeyah and the Matureedeyah specifically within their incorrect derived understanding of the subject of 'cause and affect' in the world.

- While the third group, are those who correctly affirm and implement the methodology of the people of the Sunnah and adherence to the Jamaa'ah."

(5)

THE DANGER OF INTENTIONALLY FOLLOWING AMBIGUOUS MEANINGS

Various Scholars

Imaam Ibn al-Qayyim al-Jawzeeyah, may Allaah have mercy upon him, explained to in a number of his scholastic works the different ways in which the first Muslims understood that Shaytaan's attacks and strives to lead astray the sons and daughters of Aadam. Regarding, the historical example of one misguided sect, the Khawaarij, mentioning their clear extremism despite offering many acts of worship to Allaah, [1]

"...This is the state of the sect of the Khawaarij who the people of steadfastness upon the Sunnah, would look down upon their own prayers, disdain their own fasting, and disdain their own recitation of the Qur'an, when compared to those performed of the people of this astray sect! Yet, know that both of these matters, extremism and negligence, leave the boundaries of Sunnah and are innovation. It may happen that this person goes towards innovation through negligence and neglect, while another individual goes towards innovation by going beyond the bounds and excessiveness.

Some of the scholars from the first generations of Muslims would say:

"Allaah did not establish any command to engage in a matter except that Shaytaan developed in relation to it two separate paths of temptation. Leading the worshipper either towards turning away and neglecting that command or through striving to lead them to go beyond the proper boundaries when performing it, and this is extremism." *He, Shaytaan, does not truly care through which of the two ways he succeeds in making you leave the original correct performance of that action; whether deceiving you to go towards excessiveness in that*

[1] Madaarij as-Saalikeen page 108

command or by causing a deficiency in your practice of it.

The Prophet, may Allaah's praise and salutations be upon him. said to 'Abdullah Ibn 'Amr Ibn Al-'Aas, may Allaah be pleased with him and his father,[2]

{Oh 'Abdullah, every activity has a period of vitality and strength, and every period of strength has it's low point. So the one whose low point conforms to the guidance of the Sunnah is successful, and the one whose low point conforms to some innovation in the religion is a failure and one who has lost.}

He said this to him when ordering him towards putting forth a moderate amount of deeds. As every good is found in striving towards moderation, in joining between sincerely by making the action for Allaah alone along with adherence to the Sunnah, just as some of the Companions would say,

"Limited actions upon the path and the Sunnah is better than exertions and efforts in that which differ from the path and the Sunnah."

So be diligent in making your works upon the methodology of the prophets, may Allaah praise and salutations be upon them all."

One of the pathways that leads to straying away from the guidance of the Sunnah which is often witnessed in our age is - to focus upon and following ambiguous meanings of references from the source texts of Islaam. As knowledge based dialogues and works of Sharee'ah knowledge spread and circulate today, various Muslim groups, "Islamic" thinkers, callers, and speakers are forced to reinterpret the source texts to conform to their personal

---
[2] This hadeeth with similar wording has been authenticated by Haafidh Ibn Hajr in Al-'Amaalee Al-Mutalaqah

concepts, strange pronouncements, and unsupported organizational priorities, in order to attempt to deceive the general Muslim people into believing their distortions of our revealed religion are correct.

For this reason, it is important to understand that, just as Allaah has warned us regarding the Noble Qur'aan, that our other sources of knowledge can be misinterpreted and misunderstood, when the intent or methodology of seeking their guidance used does not follow the methodology of the noble Companions, which they learned from the Messenger of Allaah, may the praise and salutations of Allaah be upon him. Sheikh Muhammad Baazmool, may Allaah preserve him, said,[3]

> *"What is generally meant by any text which is clear and unambiguous is not only the text of the Qur'aan. As a verse may be from those source texts which are ambiguous and not understood except by the scholars whereas the related hadeeth narration of the Messenger of Allaah, may the praise and salutations of Allaah be upon him, in this specific issue is clear and unambiguous. In this case the full meaning of the verse is taken from that unambiguous authentic hadeeth narration. This is the meaning of the statement of some of the people of knowledge, "The Sunnah finalizes and determines the understanding of the Book of Allaah."*
>
> *What is intended by 'unambiguous' is any source text which clearly indicates the intended Sharee'ah meaning in that matter or area. The opposite of that are those ambiguous source texts which require further clarification from the people of knowledge.*
>
> *That source text which is ambiguous might be a verse of the Qur'aan or a hadeeth narration, just like an ambiguous source texts may be either from the Book of Allaah or from the narrations of the Sunnah.*

[3] Taken from the Facebook page of Sheikh Muhammad Baazmool

An example of this is the statement of Allaah the Most High, ❖ ***Take not the Jews and the Christians as auliyaa' (friends, protectors, helpers, etc.), they are but auliyaa' to one another. And if any amongst you takes them as auliyaa', then surely he is one of them....*** ❖ *-(Surah Al-Ma'idah: 51) the apparent unexplained meaning is that anyone who loves and assists any non-Muslim, then he is considered from among them.*

Yet this explanation is not what is intended by this verse, since the other source texts of the Sharee'ah generally indicate that there may be natural love and assistance to wards a non-Muslim, that does not cause someone to become a disbeliever. Such as the love of a child for their parents who are from the non-Muslims, and his efforts in assisting and supporting them both against someone who intends them harm.

Or for example that love which a man has for his wife who is a Christian, and his protecting and defending her, and assisting her.

The Sharee'ah indicates that it is possible to support an individual non-Muslim without that being the major form of disbelief which takes a Muslim outside of the religion, just as is indicated through the authentic accounts of Haatab and Abee Lubaabah, in the time of the Companions of the messenger of Allaah, may Allaah be please with them all.

Upon this we say that since its general meaning, is not what is intended by the Sharee'ah, then this verse is considered ambiguous such that we understand its with those unambiguous evidences which indicate what the majority of the source texts indicate in this case, as we have just explained. And the success is from Allaah alone."

It is from the important weapons of arming ourselves with authentic knowledge that we are able to recognize how misguided groups and their ideological leaders who designate themselves as Muslim "thinkers" and intellectuals often distort the source texts in support their distorted concepts and principles. It is common for this or that modern Muslim individual "thinker" or one of the various Muslim groups, calling to a misguided distorted interpretation of Islaam, puts forward that certain verses have such-and-such meaning or that this hadeeth means that such-and-such is the most important aspect of Islaam. When this is encountered it is important for us all to carefully consider what does or does not support their interpretations, their underlying principles and general methodology in reaching it, as well as their possible motivations for putting for that specific explanation of the source texts of Islaam.

Correspondingly, the scholars have mentioned that this classification of unambiguous and ambiguous texts, also applies to statements of knowledge from the first generations of scholars. As many individuals now falsely claim that their "way" is what they Salaf were upon, by subtly misquoting isolated evidences or selective statements. In the same way, these claims using the statements of the first generations require careful examination in light of all related texts and evidences. This has been explained comprehensively by the esteemed Sheikh Saaleh ibn 'Abdul-'Azeez Aal-Sheikh , may Allaah preserve him. He said,[4]

---

[4] From a recorded lectured entitled 'Establishing the Origin of the Correct Beliefs Safeguards Islaam from Destructive Dangers'

"Likewise, within the actions of the Salaf, within what they did there is that which is unambiguous and clear, yet there is also that which is ambiguous and will not be understood by everyone but only properly comprehended by the scholars. Some of the people come forward in our age, and they say this issue of revolting against the rulers, and overthrowing the rulers, whom the people have given a pledge of allegiance, is one in which the Salaf did not actually have a set methodology. They assert that some of the Salaf said such-and-such permitting it and some of them said such-and-such opposing it. Then these people then transmit carefully selected statements from the Salaf from this source and that source. But this is the exact, methodology which Allaah warns us against.

As such, we must ask, how can we know what is the correct methodology of Islaam, that methodology proceeded upon by the first generations of Muslims? Know that their methodology must properly understood through considering all their statements and actions collectively. As it should be affirmed that Allaah has not made any single individual among them, or even two of them infallible from falling to an error.

*The Prophet, may Allaah's praise and salutations be upon him, made clear to us that this Ummah is the best of the nations, starting with who? Starting with the generation of the Sahaabah {**The best of you are my generation and then those who come after them then those who come after them.**} Their characteristic of merit and guidance mentioned is found with them collectively.*

For this reason. it is clear that one of the scholars of the Salaf might have slipped into a error or mistake in his position despite striving to reach the correct judgement or ruling in that issue; so his affair in this error returns back to Allaah, and he still maintains his merit as a person of knowledge, but that scholar must not ever be followed in any mistake he made. A scholar, despite us acknowledging him as indeed being a scholar, must not be unquestionably followed, which would include in any matters he is incorrect in. The general absolute following is only suitable towards the guidance of the Book of Allaah and the Sunnah.

As Allaah has not made any single individual infallible from mistakes after His Prophet, may Allaah's praise and salutations be upon him. But collectively the Muslim Ummah is infallible from all joining or agreeing upon falsehood. Since there will always be those who are guided who is standing steadfastly for Allaah with the sound proofs of the religion. This is from the most important of issues for us to understand.

Someone may come and say [The first generations did not have a methodology for this.] For instance, regarding the Sharee'ah guidelines regarding enjoining the good and forbidding wrongdoing. They wrongly say: [The first generations did not have a methodology for this!]

But where within their position, are their principles taken from the scholars like Imaam Ahmad, or the other leading scholars like Ibn Khuzaymah, Ibn Taymeeyah, and al-Barbahaaree? Where are the beliefs of these acknowledged scholars with them? From where did the Muslims learn the beliefs found in the work like al-Waasiteeyah? Where are the books of essential beliefs that such people actually refer to? Where, in their claimed way, is the sound methodology taken from the people of hadeeth? Where is the full methodology of the Salaf in what such people are upon?

What they do is simply derive a position from an individual statement of so-and-so or the statement of so-and-so, merely one or two individuals, without considering these other guiding matters. This way is in fact, that mentioned blameworthy practice of following those texts which will not be understood by everyone, only the scholars. They have turned away from the clear and unambiguous narrations, and chosen to follow those narration and reports which will not be understood by everyone, but are only properly comprehended by the people of knowledge.

Therefore, that individual who comes with a matter in the area of beliefs which practically opposes this manner of taking from their guidance of the Salaf as a whole, and differs with what has been established among the majority of them, in their understanding of the Book of Allaah and the Sunnah, regarding the matters of belief or issues of general methodology, and aspects of specific ways of doing things, and supports this by relying on isolated narrations from here and here, is clearly opposing this principle and foundation about our proper approach to texts and narrations. For this reason, this is blameworthy, meaning following those ambiguous narrations which will not be understood by everyone, other than those who are suitable scholars.

This occurs even to the degree that they, the people who follow what is ambiguous, also misconstrue hadeeth narrations. They in fact, also misinterpret hadeeth narrations. Allaah has said **...*So as for those in whose hearts there is a deviation (from the truth) they follow that which is not entirely clear thereof, seeking al-Fitnah (polytheism and trials, etc.), and seeking for its hidden meanings,*** *-(Surah Al-Imran: 7) This situation which Allaah mentions, is what we see today directly and clearly.*

If is for that reason that Allaah the Most Exalted, the Most Magnificent, said, **❦ Verily, those who divide their religion and break up into sects (all kinds of religious sects), you have no concern in them in the least. Their affair is only with Allaah, Who then will tell them what they used to do. ❦** *-(Surah Al-An'am: 159). You should have no concern for listening to these people in the slightest. Rather, stay away, and separate from them. And adhere to the sound methodology of guidance until death reaches you and you are standing upon that.*

For this reason, we see that properly adhering to the sound methodology of guidance requires integrity. It is not adhered to by arbitrarily taking from isolated independent scholastic positions, nor by conflicting with a source text with your intellect, nor by opposing the source texts as a whole, or conflicting with the establish principles of the Sharee'ah through claiming something must be accepted for a claimed 'public benefit'. Similarly, adhering to what is correct is not accomplished by conflicting with the general overall methodology of the Salaf by bringing isolated individual statements and transmissions, or advancing individually held interpretations from only a single scholar. This includes the leading scholars of the first three generations of Muslims. As it is possible that someone from among them was in a situation or circumstance that he faced, where his adopted position in fact clearly opposed the general methodology of the Salaf. This is since, he is not a prophet such that we must adopt everything single position he held!

*It is was for this reason that Imaam Maalik Ibn Anas, may Allaah the Most High, have mercy upon him, the Imam of Medinah, the city of emigration, may Allaah reward him with the best of rewards, said, **"There is not anyone from among us but we accept from his statements and we reject from his statements, except the one in this grave,"** as he indicated towards the Prophet's grave.*

Therefor, do not fail to make firm the understanding of this principle within yourselves. The principle is: the Qur'aan has verses that are unambiguous in meaning and verses which will not be understood by everyone but which are properly comprehended by the scholars. Many sects have gone astray by following those verses whose meaning was not readily apparent to everyone, and they ended up being from the seventy-two sects that will suffer in Hellfire.

Likewise in relation to the hadeeth narrations of the Prophet, there is a group of people who pursue those narrations which are ambiguous and will not be understood properly except by the scholars, while at the same time those people turn away from the narrations which are clear and unambiguous. Similarly, this is also the case of the statements and actions of the Companions of the Messenger of Allaah, as well as the statements and actions of the various scholars of the Salaf. There are those people who wrongly pursue what is ambiguous from among there statements and actions and turn away from other clear and unambiguous statements or actions. There is not any solitary matter or report which is brought forth, from other than the Prophet, which is something the general methodology of the Salaf is actually founded upon, and requires unquestioned acceptance.

This understanding is the state of soundness and sufficiency for this Ummah in its preserved guidance, and all praise is due to Allaah. This sufficiency, in their general way, relates to both taking the apparent meaning of scholastic reports that are used to derive Sharee'ah positions, and refers to the comprehensive recording and preservation of their reports and narrations. Certainly, the leading scholars of hadeeth and the leading scholars of Islaam have established a firm foundation in both of these areas for us, and they have left that for us in those books they have authored know as 'Mussanafaat'. May Allaah grant them the best of rewards and raise their level in the gardens of delight found in Paradise.

As such, be diligent in understanding this principle connected to those today who wrongly take from the ambiguous and turn away from that which is unambiguous from our religious sources. If someone comes to you who derived a position only from what can be rightly describes as an ambiguous text, narration, or action, remember what I have mentioned to you from the hadeeth **{When you see those people who follow that which is allegorical in the Qur'aan, those are the people whom Allaah has named in the Qur'aan. So avoid them.}** *and the verse* ❖**...So as for those in whose hearts there is a deviation (from the truth) they follow that which is not entirely clear thereof, seeking Al-Fitnah (polytheism and trials, etc.), and seeking for its hidden meanings**❖-*(Surah Aal-'Imraan: 7) as found within the Qur'aan.*

Know that in this same way, there are those in whose hearts is deviation who also pursue what is ambiguous, from other religious sources besides the Qur'aan. Certainly, from the reports of the Sunnah they are seen to do so seeking fitnah. Likewise in this same way, those in whose hearts there is deviation pursue what is ambiguous from the reports of the statements and actions of the Companions, seeking fitnah. And they also do the same with the narrations of the scholars of the Salaf seeking fitnah. This is what they do. All praise is due to Allaah, this topic has been made clear and explained properly."

Sheikh al-Islaam Ibn Taymeeyah, may Allaah have mercy upon him, said,[5]

"We know that the Qur'aan was recited by the Companions, and Successors, and those Muslims of the generation who were successors to the Successors, and that they were most knowledgable of its correct explanation and its intended meaning.

This is since they were those with the greatest understanding of that truth with which Allaah sent His Messenger, may the praise and salutations of Allaah be upon him. Therefore, the one who opposes them and explains the verses of the Qur'aan in a manner that contradicts or opposes their explanation, has made an error in both understanding the specific evidences, as well as in that meaning intended or generally directed to by the evidences."

---

[5] The writing of Ibn Taymeeyah entitled 'Introduction to the Principles of Tafseer': pg. 38

AMBIGUOUS MEANINGS

(6)

DON'T LET YOUR BROTHER DROWN PULL HIM TOWARDS THE SUNNAH

Various Scholars

There is a well-known knowledge based narration on the authority Ibn Wahb said, we were with Imaam Maalik, and the Sunnah was mentioned, and Imaam Maalik, may Allaah have mercy upon him, said **"The Sunnah is like the Ark of Nuh, who enters it is saved, and the one who turns away from it is drowned in misguidance."**[1] Sheikh al-Islaam Ibn Taymeeyah, may Allaah have mercy upon him, explained how being connected to the Sunnah is directly affirming the message of Tawheed carried by all the prophets and messengers of Allaah, stated,[2]

"...For this reason they used to say, "Adherence to the Sunnah saves and rescues an individual." Imaam Maalik, may Allaah have mercy upon him, said "The Sunnah is like the Ark of Nuh, who enters it is saved, and the one who turns away from it is drowned in misguidance." And this is truth.

Indeed, the Ark of Nuh was entered into by those who believed the message of the prophets and who followed their guidance, whereas those who refused to enter into it rejected the message of the messengers of Allaah.

Likewise, adherence to the Sunnah is embracing that message which has come from Allaah. As such the one who follows and adheres to it, is similar to the person who chose to enter the ark with Nuh, believing inwardly and reflecting their belief outwardly. Just like the one who refuses to follow the final revealed message, is in a similar position to the one who previously refused to follow Nuh, may Allaah peace be upon him, and refused to enter into the Ark with him."

---

[1] Narrated in Tarikh al-Baghdad: vol. 7 pg. 336, Tarikh Dimashq: vol. 9 pg. 14, and the work Dham al-Kalaam wa Ahluhu: vol. 4 pg. 124: no# 885 and it is accepted in meaning by many leading scholars upon the Sunnah

[2] Majmu'a al-Fataawa: vol 4 pg. 137

This connection to the very message of the prophets and messengers, is a reminder of why it is important to take hold of the proper perspective and knowledge based understanding of our general situation as a Muslim Ummah described by the trustworthy scholars, as they are the inheritors of those prophets and messengers. Sheikh Ibn Baaz, may Allaah have mercy upon him, said,[3]

> *"There is no doubt that bringing forth the truth and spreading it in our current age, along with the efforts to invite people to the truth is considered from those efforts or endeavors that are strange. This is due to the severity of people's distance away from Islaam and their ignorance of Islaam, along with that fact that there are relatively few callers to the truth but the numerous of callers to falsehood."*

We live in an age in which most of the people have generally turned away from the revealed message of the prophets that humanity was created for Allaah's worship alone, and many Muslims have specifically strayed away from the path of guidance that saves, rescues, and protects which is found within the pure Sunnah of the final Prophet and Messenger Muhammad, just as the Ark of Nuh saved previously. In fact for Muslim minorities, the misconceptions and doubts about our Creator's guidance are even more plentiful and supported in the lands of disbelief which are far from both the lands of Islaam and the well-known scholars. Sheikh 'Abdul-'Azeez Ibn 'Abdullah Ibn Baaz, may Allaah, the Most High, have mercy upon him and enrich his reward in the Hereafter, also advised those who wish to invite to the truth how we should generally proceed and interact with others in our current age, saying,[4]

---

[3] Majmu'a al-Fataawa wa Maqallat Sheikh Ibn Baaz: vol. 3 pg. 157-158
[4] Majmu'a' al-Fataawa wa Muqoolat vol. 8, pg. 376

> *"This present age, is an age of proceeding with gentleness, patience, and wisdom. It is not an age for harshness, since the majority of people are in a state of ignorance of many matters of the religion, heedless in their approach it, and inclined towards being occupied with worldly matters.*
>
> *Therefore it is necessary that we have patience, and required that we proceed with gentleness, in order that our efforts of calling to Allaah spread and reach the people, such that that they learn what is correct. We ask Allaah to grant all of us guidance to and upon the truth."*

By Allaah's mercy in our current age, the authentic knowledge of Islaam continues to slowly spread throughout our world combating misconceptions, ignorance, and followed desires. This is among the Muslims of this Ummah, as well as non-Muslims bringing new people into the mercy of Islaam. He, Sheikh Ibn Baaz, may Allaah have mercy upon him, indicated clearly that,[5]

> *"What is legislated in Islaam is that when a Muslim hears a statement that is of benefit, that he conveys it to others. The same applies to a Muslimah, she should convey to others whatever she hears of sound knowledge. This is due to the statement of the Prophet, may the praise and salutations of Allaah be upon him, {**Convey from me even if it is a single statement.**} And he, may the praise and salutations of Allaah be upon him, if he addressed the people, said, {**Let those who are present convey to those who are absent. For perhaps the one to whom it is conveyed will understand it better than the one who first hears it.**}'*

---

[5] Majmu'a al-Fataawa wa Maqalaat, vol. 4 pg. 45

Our discerning Salafee scholars have discussed the correct perspective and approach to calling other to what is correct based upon the guidance of revelation. Their discussions provide us with detailed guidance as to how, for that Muslim who does not fear for themselves falling into confusion, our interactions should be with those who have ignorance or misconceptions.

In the past the leading scholars upon the Sunnah were clear in their efforts to distinguish and separate from the callers from among the people of innovations while at the same time, seeking to spread the Sunnah among the common deceived Muslims who may come back to the true understanding of the religion of Islaam. The scholars have openly clarified that there is a clear difference between the staunch stubborn follower of a path of misguidance, a caller or leader of misguidance, and the common Muslim who has been unknowingly deceived into believing that they stand upon what is correct. By this is intended those who have not reached the level of being willful innovators due to the proof being established against them according to the guidelines of the people of the Sunnah, nor those specific individual who the scholars state should be boycotted due to some harm they cause among the Muslims.

It is a fact that many general Muslims, especially among the minority communities in western countries, have not had anyone with even a degree of authentic knowledge gently direct and encourage them towards the Sunnah and the scholars of the Sunnah. This can be can be done, by Allaah permission, without entering into the mistake of unstructured debating, fruitless arguing, or accepting their errors and adopting their misconceptions. The guiding scholar Sheikh Ibn Baaz, may Allaah have mercy upon him, indicated why this is important today,[6]

---

[6] Majmu'a al-Fataawa vol.6 pg. 67

"It is required that we be diligent in the spreading of Sharee'ah knowledge with every type effort and with strength, otherwise the people of falsehood will continue to spread their falsehood. Therefore be concerning with benefiting the Muslims in the affairs of their religion and in their worldly well-being."

Additionally, if that misguided common person was raised within an extreme misguided sect who has reached the level of disbelief, such as the Druze in the Middle East or for example the so called "Nation of Islam" of Elijah Poole in the United States, then we are actually calling them to enter true Islaam. As an example of this, Ibn Taymeeyah, may Allaah have mercy upon him, said,[7]

"The first generations of Muslims, and the leading scholars throughout the centuries stated the evidenced declaration of the disbelief of the sect of the Jahmeeyah generally and broadly altogether, but as for the ruling of general individuals connected to them, then they supplicated for their eventual guidance away from falsehood and would asked Allaah for to forgiveness that person."

Sheikh Muqbil was asked, **"There are those, who have been affected by the extreme methodology of Mahmood al-Haddad, that say you support them in their position that anyone who falls into something of innovation is generally considered and innovator. They say that you, yourself mentioned this in the cassette "Questions from the Young Men of Shabwah. What do you say in response to this claim?"** He clarified, may Allaah have mercy upon him, saying[8]

"We say, a man who is a Sunnee, if he falls into a specific matter in religious innovation, then we rule upon that action, that the action itself, is one of innovation. But

---

[7] Bayaan Talbees al-Jahmeeyah: vol. 1 pg. 10
[8] From the audio cassette Questions from the People of Tahham

as for the man himself, then we are not able to generally rule that he is a innovator, rather it may be that matter is overcome and swallowed by his merits..."

The scholar Sheikh Hammad Al-Ansaaree, may Allaah have mercy upon him, stated we explain and clarify to them the truth,[9]

"For the one who falls into practicing an innovation, we initially say to him. 'What your doing is the actions of those of someone who has innovated and changed the religion.' But if he is obstinate and continues upon that, thereafter we eventually say. 'You are an innovator in the religion.'"

There is clear advice from the scholars showing that it important to treat the general Muslims according to their outwardly shown position of truly desiring Islaam, whenever there are no statements or actions which shows an intentional or stubborn support of misguidance or an strong attachment to religious innovation and falsehood. The following is an example of how the scholars of the Sunnah differentiate between the ignorant follower and the stubborn opposer to the guidance of the Sunnah. Sheikh Muqbil Ibn Haadee, may Allaah have mercy upon him, was asked, **"What should our position be towards those Muslims who affiliate themselves to these different modern parties and ideological orientations? Do we accept them absolutely, or do we reject them absolutely? Or do we accept and support them and reject and disassociate ourselves from them, according to the specific degree of good and evil and wrongdoing that we find them upon? Do we generally turn away and abandon them, due to their affiliations to these groups or not? May Allaah, the Most High, bless you."** He, replied,[10]

---

[9]   Majmu'a Fatawaa of Sheikh Hamaad Al-Ansaaree vol.2 pg. 482
[10] Fataawa ID 4580 from muqbel.net

"As for our general allegiance and support, then we consider them to be from the Muslims. This is since, that despite that they are those who have wrongly turned towards democracy, they are considered Muslims, but misguided. If you met one of them you give him the greetings of salaams, 'Assalaamu aleikum wa rahmatAllaah'. If he offers you the greeting, then you respond, 'Wa aleikum assalaam wa rahmatAllaah'. But you do not attend their lectures, nor take part in their gatherings, and do not busy yourself with that misguidance they are upon.

Since I returned back to Yemen, which is close to seventeen years or more. It has not been seen that significant numbers of people have affiliated themselves with those groups associated, here in Yemen, with the Muslim Brotherhood organization, they have not increased nor decreased among the general people. The reason for this is that they, that organization, are primarily concerned with gaining positions of governmental power, as well as being focused upon collecting people's money...

In a similar question which is directly connected to understanding this distinction, Sheikh Muhammad Baazmool, was asked, **Question: Are those people from among general Muslims considered to be those following the first generations when they allow their beards to grow, shorten their thobes to what is recommended by the Sharee'ah, adhere to some of the authentic practices of the Sunnah, and struggle within themselves to be steadfast? Are they then considered to be those people following the first three generations, or is this description only to be used for those who additionally commit themselves to seeking knowledge upon the way of the Salaf as Muslims?**

Answer: The fundamental assumption is that such common Muslims who sincerely follow the Qur'aan and Sunnah, follow the way of the first generations in a broad sense. Since they do, in general, believe that it is a requirement for every Muslim to adhere to the guidance of the Messenger of Allaah, may Allaah's praise and salutations be upon him, and to follow the path of the Companions in how they adhered to his guidance which was conveyed to them. This is the fundamental assumption.

It is for this reason that the common Muslims are naturally closer to their Muslim brothers who knowingly and specifically follow the first three distinguished generations, then they are to the people specifically upon of innovation and the following of their desires among the Ummah. We see that, for the most part, when a general Muslim who in some aspect of his practice does something which opposes to the correct methodology and believer's way, and you inform him of what is in fact the evidenced truth, then generally he then accepts this and follows the truth of that matter. Because he knows that adhering to this way, the way of the Messenger and his Companions, is undoubtedly the only straight path of Allaah.

Additionally, for that general Muslim who wrongly shaves down or removes his beard, or allows his garment to hang below his ankles, but he nonetheless remains upon the clear foundation of sincerely affirming the requirement of following the Messenger of Allaah and following the believer's way of his noble Companions, then despite his sin and opposition to what is the correct ruling in those issues he is in error regarding, he is considered a Salafee -with deficiencies- due to those matters that he stands in error or has transgressed regarding.

On the other hand, you will also find from among the people that man who shortens the length of his thobe and allows his beard to grow long, yet in reality he is an misguided astray individual who has in fact deviated and drifted far away from the straight path.

Indeed, this reality was something in fact mentioned by the Messenger of Allaah, may Allaah's praise and salutations be upon him, when he informed the Companions that there would be some people who recited the Qur'aan but it would not truly go beyond their throats. He further mentioned about those people that one of Muslims would dismiss and disparage his own performance of ritual prayer when compared to these people, he was mentioning, and their extensive prayer, and likewise dismiss and consider little his own fasting, when compared next to the extensive fasting of these people. Yet those being mentioned and referred to are the astray sect of the Khawaarij.

Take note that, despite these apparently righteous actions of worship they would perform, the Messenger Of Allaah, nevertheless said about them, due to their innovation, **{If I were to encounter these people, I would wipe them out and destroy them just the people of 'Ad were completely wiped out and destroyed.}** *And the successes from Allaah."*

This understanding was further clarified by the sheikh himself Sheikh Muhammad Baazmool, in a question directed to him, **"From what has been published from you previously is the statement "Not every Muslim is upon the way of the first three generations. Those people who are engaging in innovated matters and aspects of misguidance, if that does not reach the level of what removes someone from the religion, then they are included in those identified a the people of**

Islaam. However they are not considered from among those described as Salafee or following the first three generations." Yet elsewhere you stated:

"The fundamental assumption is that such common Muslims who sincerely follow the Qur'aan and Sunnah, follow the way of the first generations in a broad sense. Since they, do in generally believe that it is a requirement for every Muslim to adhere to the guidance of the Messenger of Allaah, may Allaah's praise and salutations be upon him, and to follow the path of the Companions in how they adhered to his guidance which was conveyed to them. This is the fundamental assumption. It is for this reason that the common Muslims are naturally closer to their Muslim brothers who knowingly and specifically follow the first three distinguished generations, then they are to the people specifically upon of innovation and the following of their desires among the Ummah." How can we dispel any contradiction that seems to be between these two statements?" [11]

"I replied, "The is no contradiction, nor any conflict between these two, if Allaah so wills.

As, the fundamental assumption is that a common Muslim broadly follows the Salaf. This is because the very meaning of Islaam is to follow the the Messenger of Allaah, may Allaah's praise and salutations be upon him, adhere to his guidance, and take what comes from the Companions as the religion. This is the foundation and original position.

However, not every Muslim remains upon this original position. Therefor not every Muslim, in how he proceeds in Islaam, is a Salafee. He may fall into matters which oppose and go against what the Messenger of Allaah, and his Companions stood upon, but this does not take

---

[11] Taken from the Facebook page of Sheikh Muhammad Baazmool

him outside of Islaam!

For this reason that Muslim who, within his heart, hasn't embraced false desires or religious innovations, such that whenever it is properly explained to him that whatever he holds which opposes what the Messenger of Allaah, may Allaah's praise and salutations be upon him, and his Companions practiced as Islaam, he will leave it and abandon that innovated matter and turn towards the Sunnah. This is a reality which we have witness and seen among the common Muslims.

So we can say that common Muslims follow the first generation generally, but not all individually, from the aspect of their remaining upon the original natural of compliance with and acceptance of Allaah's guidance. However, every individual Muslim is not Salafee from the aspect of the reality that individually and personally. A specific person may have incorrect matters in his practice of the religion which oppose the evidenced guidance of Islaam, according to whatever level of opposition he specifically has reached of misguidance. And the success is from Allaah."

Alhamdulillah, we have specific detailed advice from the well known steadfast scholars of how to encourage our brothers and sisters, who are just general Muslims. The scholars have explained that it is possible to generally encourage Muslims toward adherence to the Jamaa'ah and warning them against innovation by calling to the revealed sources, especially in those places and times in which those engaged in doing so are few and far between.

Sheikh Rabee'a' Ibn Haadee, may Allaah preserve him, was asked,[12] ***"Is it permissible for someone to work to invite the people to the way of the first generations in his village or area, but do so without making apparent that he is from those who proceed upon this methodology, until some of them accept him and his efforts? This being done in light of the fact that he is still inviting them to the truth."***

Answer: "The caller does not need to say to them, 'I am Salafee, I am Salafee.' But he could say to them, "This is the guidance of Book of Allaah and the Sunnah of the Messenger of Allaah..." And invites them towards this. It is not a requirement that he says to them, "I am Salafee." But he can say to them, "This is the guidance of Book of Allaah and the Sunnah of the Messenger of Allaah..." and in that way he teaches them sound knowledge.

Yet if he, was perhaps pressured or compelled to say to them, "I am not Salafee," then in this case, we say it is required that he state clearly that he is upon the way of the first generations."

Sheikh Ubayd Ibn 'Abdullah al-Jaabiree, may Allaah preserve him, was similarly asked,[13] ***"Some individuals hold that it is not suitable to initially warn the general Muslims away from specific individuals of innovation, as they probably won't accept such warnings that criticize those accepted individuals. Rather, they assert that we gradually work with them by teaching them what is the Sunnah and what is innovation generally, such that when they come to properly understand that initially, then afterwards we can later mention to then the specific names of those innovating individuals. Is this assertion <u>correct and sound</u>?***

[12] Taken from the audio lecture: A Comfortable Sitting in Ranks." from the Sheikh's website Question # 199
[13] From the lecture "From the Matters Leading to Allaah Loving His Worshiper." part of the series Salafi Gatherings in Qatar.

Answer: Yes, this is correct, and it is what we stand and proceed upon if Allaah the Most High so wills. Since, from the characteristics of our call, meaning the call of the people of the Sunnah and the Jamaa'ah, is using wisdom. This is just as Allaah, the Most High, said to His Prophet, may Allaah's praise and salutations be upon him, yet the meaning is addressed to the Muslims generally, it generally encompasses everyone striving to call to Allaah upon knowledge and insight, He said., ❦ **Invite (mankind, O Muhammad) to the Way of your Lord (i.e. Islaam) with wisdom (i.e. with the Divine Inspiration and the Qur'aan) and fair preaching...** ❦ *-(Surah An-Nahl: 125) Furthermore, Alee, may Allaah be pleased with him, said,* **"Speak to the people in a way and with what they will understand."**

It is upon a person striving in calling to Allaah upon knowledge and insight to consider the issues of related to achieving the greater collective good and preventing the greater overall harm among the Muslims. If the people in your country have a deep seated love of a specific individual, such that he is considered their leader who is followed and they do not know the matters of Islaam except through him, yet the caller sees, with evidence, that this individual is a misguided innovator, he should not directly say anything about him.

Rather cultivate within those general people a love of the Sunnah and the people of the Sunnah, and warn them away from innovation in a general way. For example, saying 'This matter is something innovated into Islaam and 'This is something innovated into Islaam, and this other matter is also something newly innovated into the religion,' until the clear comprehension of these fundamentals are fostered within them, and their hearts are satisfied with their correctness and soundness. This is the proper way to clarifies this to them.

As for the person who simply starts with declaring "This practice is a incorrect." or who does not take into consideration that from the heads of the people of innovation whom they might be warning against in that land, may be someone with governmental responsibility, such as the minister for religious affairs, or a minister of justice, or the chief judge of that land. Since for individuals in these positions in society it is not suitable to publicly warn the general people against them, as this usually only harms our general efforts to call them to Allaah, and doesn't produce any overall benefit.

*It is found in Saheeh al-Bukhaaree in an hadeeth on the authority of 'Aishah, may Allaah be pleased with her, said, A man asked for permission to visit the Prophet, may the praise and salutations of Allaah be upon him, and the Prophet said, {**Give him permission, yet he is an evil brother of his tribe.**} Yet when the man entered he spoke politely to him. I said, "Messenger of Allaah, you said what you said about him, but then spoke politely to him?" He said, {**Oh A'ishah. The worst of people is the one people leave alone or avoid fearing his coarseness or foul words.'**} He said, {**Oh A'ishah, the worst of people is the one people leave alone or avoid fearing his coarseness or foul words.**}*

Therefore some of the people, you do not boycott, nor do you warn against them, because the evil which may come from him due to undertaking that with them specifically, will ultimately cause greater harm to the people upon Islaam generally.

As for the case of the average person who falls into a personal mistake or error in the religion, if when he is spoken to, he accepts and heeds that advice, then good. Otherwise, if it is warranted in that case, he may be boycotted, and no longer treated with honor or respect."

It is seen from some Muslims, that they practically hold that a general Muslim whom we outwardly see has a clearly incorrect religious understanding or position should immediately be turned away from and not interacted with in any circumstance. This is indeed correct for the one who fears for his religion being harmed by interacting with that individual with errors. But a lack of knowledge of the detailed statements of the scholars in this issue often prevents someone upon steadfastness in his religion from directing another general Muslim, who is not a stubborn opposer to the Sunnah, toward correcting and strengthening their understanding and practice of Islaam through a brief word or statement of authentic knowledge from the source texts or the scholars. As Sheikh al-'Utheimeen, may Allaah have mercy upon him, mentioned,[14]

> *"Do not demean your brother Muslim, even if he doesn't understand a very simple issue in the religion, still do not belittle him. As perhaps Allaah will open a way for him coming to understand, and lead him to gaining such knowledge that he will become more knowledgeable than you."*

We find guidance in the statements of our scholars who proceed upon the way of the first generations which indicates that those Muslims who strive to gain authentic knowledge to rectify themselves and their families, can also play a role and have a clear contribution to make in encouraging their general brothers and sisters to better learn and practice Islaam. Because, even after some Muslims come to openly affirm the soundness of the methodology of the first generations, it is still necessary to continue to patiently advise, support, and assist the one you see sincerely moving toward the way of the Salaf. Sheikh Rabee'a Ibn Haadee, may Allaah preserve him, was

---

[14] His Explanation of the poem of Ibn al-Qayyim an-Nooneeyah: pg. 421

asked, *"If a man accepted and now strives to proceed on the methodology of the first three generations, but he still has or reflects some of the harmful effects of his previous misguidance, do we overlook this until he becomes firm upon the way of the Salaf?"* The Sheikh replied,[15]

"Yes, we overlook that, explaining and clarifying to him what he is failing to do which he should be, which is leading to him continuing to be religiously weak, and leading to him remaining upon the effect of his previous history. Explain to him, clarify this to him, and direct him towards those books that through his reading them will enable him to refine and correct himself. Because this past history of error has caused damage.

Specifically, concerning someone raised within this land where the correct methodology is clear, he doesn't have an excuse to continue to be weak and unsteady in the religion. Yet we still help him develop, and take the needed time with him, be patient with him, may Allaah bless you with good, until he reaches a stage of true betterment and rectification."

This is also what is found among the earlier scholars of the current age. Sheikh 'Abdur-Rahman as-Sa'dee, may Allaah have mercy upon him, said about the positive effects of someone keeping company with the Muslims who are righteous[16]

"The goodness which reaches a worshiper through his sitting with a righteous Muslim is more significant and more virtuous than the wonderful smell of fine musk. Certainly such a person will teach you that which will benefit you, whether in regard to your religious or his worldly affairs, or he will direct you towards good by offering sound advice, or he will warn you from placing

[15] Audio lecture: The Path to Victory and Dominion dated 03-25-1422
[16] Baheejatul-Quloob al-'Abraar, vol. 1 pg. 156

himself upon some matter that which will inevitably bring harm to you.

Such a person encourages you upon the obedience of Allaah, upon treating your parents with goodness, upon maintaining familiarity ties and relations, and gives you insight into your own shortcomings and failings. He invites you to having the excellence of and to stand upon having the best of character, whether this be in your statements, your actions, or you general situation and state."

Which of us as Muslims doesn't want this for ourselves, so how can we not seek that for our brothers, when undertaken upon the guidance of the Sunnah. This is why a mountain on knowledge in our age, Sheikh Muhammad Ibn Saaleh al-'Utheimeen, may Allaah have mercy upon him, said generally,[17]

"An individual should offer advice to every Muslim in a way that deals with them the same way he deals with himself, and the same way he would like for the people to deal with him. He doesn't lie against them, he doesn't forsake him, he doesn't mislead him, he doesn't deceive him, nor is he disloyal to another Muslim.

Rather he stands with him as someone offering advice from any direction. If his brother ask for his advice about a matter, then it is obligatory upon him to direct his brother towards whatever it is he holds as best for the rectification and good state of his religious and worldly affairs."

Just as a past mountain of knowledge from our Salaf, 'Abdullah Ibn al-Mubaarak, may Allaah have mercy upon him, said,[18]

---

[17] Commentary on Riyadh as-Saaliheen: vol. 5 pg. 252
[18] Rawdahul- Uqalaa' of Ibn Hibaan: vol 1 pg. 196

"It used to be that when a man saw from his Muslim brother that blameworthy matter which he disliked, he would tell him to hide this matter, and then he would privately criticize him and tell me to stop engaging in that matter. Such that he was given a reward for the person hiding that, and he would be rewarded for his admonition for him to stop that blameworthy matter.

But as for today, is someone sees someone from anyone which he considered blameworthy, he becomes furious with him, and exposes his secret."

Sheikh al-'Utheimeen, may Allaah have mercy upon him, also said,[19]

"A Muslim brother it is required to be someone who gives advice to his Muslim brother, directing him toward what is good, clarifying that to him, and inviting him to it."

This is true because as, Sheikh Saaleh Ibn Fauzaan, may Allaah preserve him, said,[20]

"A good word directed toward someone will certainly have some positive effect upon an individual. Even if, at a minimum, it only slightly reduces his harm or wrongdoing, and guide him towards a position where he is more likely to accept the truth."

Although your contribution may not be teaching classes, yet it can easily be a beneficial word based upon sure knowledge you possess directed to your general Muslim brother or sister. Sheikh al-'Utheimeen, may Allaah have mercy upon him, explained situations similar this in relation to those who were Muslim teachers in a school but not from the people of knowledge. He was asked, **"May Allaah direct good towards you. We are teachers and often questions are directed to us, so we answer**

---
[19] Sharh Riyadh as-Saaliheen: vol. 2 pg. 383
[20] Conclusive Answers to Doubts and Misconceptions that Have Arisen pg. 43

according to the knowledge we have. Is this considered giving rulings, and acting haphazardly toward Allaah, the Most Glorified and the Most Exalted?" and responded saying, [21]

> "*If your responses are according to what you know is the truth, then it is not acting or speaking haphazardly.*

Questioner: Are we acting like someone in the position of a mufti, meaning a scholar rightfully issuing a religious rulings, when we answer them?

Sheikh al-'Utheimeen replied: The messenger of Allaah said, {Convey from me even if it is a single statement.} meaning speaking about that which you individually are certain about, otherwise do not speak.

Questioner: Meaning when speaking about a ruling that is clear and apparent?

Sheikh al-'Utheimeen replied: For example, if a student asks you saying, 'What do you say about fornication?' You should say, 'It is forbidden.' There is no problem conveying this. But not if he asks you about an issue which is not fully understood, except by someone who is at a minimum a student of knowledge. If you are unsure or uncertain whether a matter is permissible or not, and you still speak in this situation, stating a ruling, then this is something not permissible for you to do. But as for what is clear, then it is something clear to convey.

Questioner: The problem is about possibly not conveying knowledge of a ruling at the time a questioner asks. The one who is asked is generally aware of the ruling, but is not entirely sure about it maybe due to forgetting the evidence supporting it. Should someone speak then for example?

---

[21] Audio file in the voice of the Sheikh from http://binothaimeen.net

Sheikh al-'Utheimeen replied: No, rather wait and say to the student, 'Just wait until I have a chance to research this, or until I can ask someone of knowledge.' Since, while that statement about religious matters remain unspoken and within you, you still hold it and have control over it. But as soon as you allow that statement to be spoken out, now you no longer have any control over it."

Sheikh al-'Utheimeen, may Allaah have mercy upon him, was also asked, **Question: I am a young man who wants to be a caller to Allaah, but I do not possess the proper manners necessary for this. Is the publishing and distribution of beneficial Islamic books or an Islamic tapes sufficient for this? Please advise me, may Allaah reward you with good.** He said in response,[22]

"Yes, there is no doubt that if a person does not have the ability to call to Allaah as an individual, then it is certainly possible for him to call to Allaah through the distribution of beneficial books and tapes. However, because this is being done on the basis of, or because of his not having the ability to call to Allaah as an individual, then he should not distribute books or tapes except after presenting them for examination to a student of knowledge who would be aware of what might be in them from mistakes of errors.

This is in order to prevent that person from distributing material that contains mistakes when he has not been advised or become aware of this. Additionally from the methods of calling to Allaah is to come to agreement with a student of knowledge that he produce material that invites to that which is beneficial and good, and that you pay for the expenses of that effort."

---

[22] From 'Islamic Rulings': Vol. 4, Page 284

As a clear encouragement for every Muslim from the general Muslim men and women to spread the Sunnah upon evidence and clarity Sheikh al-'Utheimeen, may Allaah have mercy upon him, explained that we are rewarded for even a little authentic Sharee'ah knowledge that we spread among our brothers and sisters. He, may Allaah have mercy upon him, said explaining the authentic hadeeth *{If the son of Aadam dies, his actions are ended except for three…knowledge by which others benefit.},*[23]

"From the benefits of this hadeeth narration, is that is not a condition that this knowledge mentioned be of a great amount. Because the Arabic form of the word, {knowledge}, is indefinite conveying a general unrestricted meaning.

This means knowledge without any conditions or restrictions, meaning any knowledge conveyed by which others benefit. Your conveying of that will benefit you after your death, even if you just helped someone learn what were the affirmed sunnah prayers regularly prayed before and after the five obligatory ritual prayers. or helped someone learn a single authentic act of the Sunnah, whether a statement or action, that someone should engage in during the ritual prayer. That effort will benefit you after your death, and you will receive a continuing reward for that.

So as mentioned, from the aspects of what is indicated in the meaning of this narration is that {..knowledge by which others benefit.} is understood to be general. It does not say, "significant knowledge". For this reason, any knowledge by which others benefit, even if it is just a little, then this is written down for the person who conveyed it, as something which they will be rewarded for after their death."

---

[23] Fath Dheel- Jalaal wa -al-Ikraam: vol. 4 pg. 38

This reflected what our Salaf, the first generation of the Muslim Ummah believed, as Ibn al-Mubaarak, may Allaah have mercy upon him, it reported to have said,[24]

> " I do not know of any level of excellence, after the excellent merit of the prophets of Allaah, greater than a person spreading knowledge."

Speaking about the sincere Muslim who has authentic knowledge and the capability to convey it in the proper way, Sheikh Muhammad 'Amman al-Jaamee , may Allaah have mercy upon him said,[25]

> "Conveying knowledge is an obligation, which stands as an individual obligation in our current time, due to the significant amount of confusion, haphazard statements, deceptions, and different form of misguidance which are present today."

Indeed, calling our brothers and sisters to the Sunnah is calling them to Allaah and to His guidance or Islaam as it is intended to be practiced. Without question, Islaam is the Sunnah and the Sunnah is Islaam. This is something there is a tremendous need for in our age as mentioned by Sheikh al-Jaame'a', may Allaah have mercy upon him. Similarly Sheikh 'Abdur-Rahman as-Sa'dee, may Allaah have mercy upon him, said,[26]

> "The endeavor of calling to Allaah and to the testimony that there is none worthy of worship other than Allaah is something generally required from everyone, meaning with each person being obligated according to the degree of his ability and capacity to do so. With the obligation upon the one who is a scholar to explain, call to, and guide others towards it more significant than what is upon the person who is not a scholar.

---

[24] Tareekh Dimashq: vol. 22 pg. 455
[25] His explanation of al'Aqeedahatul-Waaseeteyyah pg. 276
[26] al-Qawl as-Sadeed, vol. 1 pg. 44

Moreover, the obligation upon the one possess the capacity to undertake this with his body, his hand, his wealth, or his statements is greater than upon the one who lacks that capability.

*As Allaah the Most High has said, "**Fear Allaah, as much as you are able.**" Allaah has mercy upon the one who helps and aids this religion even if they are do so with even a short statement. Likewise there is only ruin for the worship who abandons whatever effort he could put forward to call to this true religion."*

Sheikh al 'Utheimeen, may Allaah have mercy upon him, said, also reminded us of the many places knowledge can and should be conveyed by Muslims,[27]

"It is necessary that a person bring forth within themselves and have the intention of gaining closeness to Allaah, the Most Glorified and the Most Exalted, in that speech which he puts forward, in order that he will be rewarded for whatever he says whether extensive or a brief word.

This intention should be there in whatever you say: to your own soul, what you say to the members of your family, what you say to your friends and associates, what you say to anyone at all from the people, if you do so seeking the Face of Allaah alone, then Allaah will reward you in whatever good you say."

How much good can be achieved by simply directing your Muslim brother or sister towards the clear statements of the scholars upon the Sunnah, and generally warning them against the people of innovation present today, while neither slipping into argumentation, nor choosing to neglect the offering of sincere advice to one who is unaware of the misguidance of their position or the error of the position of the one whom they are wrongly taking

[27] His explanation of Riyaadh as-Saaliheen, vol. 1 pg. 60

their religion from. We should each strive to convey authentic knowledge according to the guidelines of that knowledge, in permissible ways, to the very clear limits of our personal level of knowledge, to our Muslim brothers and sisters around us who sincerely love Allaah and His Messenger. This is especially true in this age where there is tremendous ignorance about true beliefs and practices of Islaam and limited callers upon clarity of belief and methodology, as some of the leading scholars such as Sheikh Ibn Baaz, may Allaah have mercy upon him, have stressed.

It is an excellent closing reminder offered to us by within the words of Sheikh al-'Utheimeen, may Allaah have mercy upon him, when he stated,[28]

> *"It is not permissible for us to easily cause divisions among the people of Allaah's religion, and the sincere worshippers of Allaah. Meaning in relation to some of us improperly rushing to declare each other as astray, or haphazardly declaring others as innovators.*
>
> *Rather if we see from one of our Muslim brothers something which opposes us in what is know to be correct from the direction of sound beliefs, or in relation to statements he makes, or actions he does. It is required that, if he is someone will less knowledge than us, then we then offer him advice, and similarly if he is someone at our same level of understanding , that we discuss and clarify this matter properly with him.*
>
> *We do not simply throw him behind our back, walk away, and then proceed to go talk about him among other people, simply leaving him misguided, such that more separations occur between the Muslims."*

---

[28] Explanation of Bulugh al-Maraam: vol. 15 pg. 285

Whenever possible, upon the guidance of the Book and the Sunnah, as explained by our noble scholars, following in the footsteps of the first three generations, without entering into fruitless debate and controversy, nor weakening your religion, or strengthening the people of misguidance. Don't simply let your confused brother or sister who generally loves the Sunnah continue to drown in misconceptions of the ignorant nor the subtle deceptions of the people of innovation, but quietly strive to pull them towards the Sunnah even with a single sound statement of gentle advice or word of clarity from a scholar. As Ibn Rajab, may Allaah have mercy upon him said,[29]

> *"The righteous first generations of Muslims when they wanted to offer advice to someone they would admonish him privately. This was to the degree that some of them would say 'The one who admonishes his brother, by speaking privately between him and his brother, then this is offering advice. While the one who admonishes his brother in front of all of the people is only rebuking and belittling him."*

And Allaah knows best. We ask Allaah for success in the affairs of our worldly lives and for success in the true life of the Hereafter, for ourselves and for every Muslim man and Muslim woman.

---

[29] Jaamee' al-Ulum al-Hikaam . pg 77

(7)

MODERN SCHOLARS WHO ARE CARRIERS OF THE FLAG OF CRITICISM AND COMMENDATION IN OUR RELIGION

Various Scholars

The noble sheikh Sheikh Zayd Ibn Haadee al-Madkhalee, may Allaah have mercy upon him, in response to a question directed to him, specifically indicated who were some of these scholars who distinguish between the people who connect them selves to Islaam and its knowledge, saying, [1]

*"....As for your question, oh questioner, **"Is it correct or not, to say in our age about a person or about several people in our land of the Kingdom of Saudi Arabia, 'So and so is the one who carries the flag of criticism and commendation?'"***

I say to you, yes it is correct to say that in this age there are several people who are those who hold and carry the flag of criticism and commendation. They are recognized by their attention and focus upon the Noble Book of Allaah and the knowledge found in its various sciences. Additionally, they are recognized by the attention and focus they give to the pure Sunnah and its various sciences, both spreading its guidance and defending it.

Allaah has blessed them with sound comprehension of Islaam generally, a firm understanding of how to call and invite to this religion, as well as sound perception of the events that are occurring among Muslims specifically. As such, there is nothing to prevent me from mentioning, in brief, some examples of those considered among these carriers, while limiting it to those who are presently alive [2]:

1. Sheikh Saaleh Fauzaan al-Fauzaan

2. Sheikh 'Abdul-'Azeez Aal-Sheikh

---
[1] From 'Responses Upon Transmitted Guidance to Questions Related to The Methodology of Islaam, pgs. 59-60
[2] Intending by this those alive at the time the Sheikh made the statement, may Allaah have mercy upon him.

3. *Sheikh Saaleh al-Luhaydaan*

4. *Sheikh 'Abdullah Al-Ghudyaan,*

5. *Sheikh Ahmad an-Najmee*

6. *Sheikh Rabee'a Ibn Haadee al-Madkhalee*

7. *Sheikh 'Abdul-Muhsin al-'Abbaad*

8. *Sheikh Saaleh ibn 'Abdul-'Azeez Aal-Sheikh*

9. *Sheikh 'Ubayd al-Jaabiree*

10. *Sheikh Saaleh as-Suhaymee*

11. *Sheikh Muhammad Ibn Haadee al-Madkhalee*

12. *Sheikh Sulaymaan Ibn 'Abdullah Abaa al-Khayl* [3]

Regarding these noble scholars, there is not anyone from among them except that he has praiseworthy efforts is preserving and protecting the Sunnah and the knowledge of the various sciences related to it, as well as defending it, along with having blessed efforts in refuting the innovated sects, that are spread among people in the world. They are those who give diligent attention to the conveying correct beliefs and properly establishing the tremendous methodology of Islaam.

Additionally, I ask that those other scholars, those whom I have not mentioned their names along with the names of the above noble scholars, to excuse me. Since they, those not mentioned, are certainly the partners and associates of these mentioned scholars, and they are those who certainly stand as beneficial skillful hands assisting in giving the needed attention to the Sunnah and refuting the people who have turned to following their desires in the religion, those who have proceeded upon deviated

---

[3] For an additional discussion of also reliable scholars please refer to 'Course Appendix 5: Know From Whom You Are Taking Your Religion From! by Sheikh Saaleh Ibn Sa'ad as-Suhaymee', which is found in Book 1. of this course series

concepts and distorted understandings. As my intent in naming these specific scholars is only to present examples of such scholars."

Sheikh Ubayd al-Jaabiree, may Allaah preserve him, clarifies the misguidance of those who in various ways restrict taking knowledge to only a few specific scholars when he was asked,[4] ***Question: Some of the people, may Allaah preserve you, say we will only take knowledge from the following major scholars: Sheikh Ibn Baaz, Sheikh al-Albaanee, and Sheikh al-'Utheimeen. So what is your advice regarding this position?***

Answer: Firstly, I say I consider these three scholars Sheikhs of Islaam of this present age of ours, and that they are leading scholars. However, secondly, the Prophet, may Allaah's praise and salutations be upon him, described the scholars as being the inheritors of the prophets. This is something considered general for every age and region of the earth, for every time and place. Such that whenever you find those scholars who are steadfast upon sound knowledge and they advise the people in what is correct, teaching them the religion of Allaah from the Book of Allaah and authentic Sunnah, then it is obligatory to take from them. Placing a restriction on taking only from certain scholars is not allowed, placing such a restriction is not something permissible.

As indeed during the time of the Salaf, first three generations, it is affirmed that some of the people would seek rulings from those major scholars from the generation of Successors of the Companions, when the Companions of the Messenger of Allaah, may Allaah be pleased with them, were there present among them. Yet there was no rejection from the Companions of the people doing so. Yet we should understand, from the guidance

---

[4] From a recorded sitting in the city of Mecca which was dated the 30th of Jumada al-Awwal in the year 1431

of our leading scholars, that if a sitting has within it two scholars, then the lesser scholar or the scholar with less knowledge, leaves speaking in that sitting to the one who is more knowledgeable than him. But this discretionary restriction is done without the obligation of restricting it.

Thereafter, and all praise is due to Allaah, from His favor is the presence of the brothers and the sons of those three noble scholars, all of whose status in knowledge no one denies. They are now present among you. But the people of desires can never refrain from working to cause separation between the scholars and the general Muslims, and they do so through every available means.

Moreover this mentioned statement throws to the side the fact that the brothers in scholastic level and excellence of those three noble scholars, as well as their students and their sons in knowledge, were already those who used to openly put forth statements of knowledge, statements which were, all praise is due to Allaah, considered sound and reliable, during the the time when those three specific scholars themselves were still alive. Yes."

In a complimentary discussion identifying some of the different scholars of the present century of our Ummah who are defending and calling to the Sunnah, the following statements is from Sheikh Rabee'a Ibn Haadee, may Allaah preserve him. It is directed at Salmaan al-'Awdah, may Allaah guide him, one of the callers towards a general intellectual chaos and lack of clarity in our religion that characterizes many modern day "callers". Like many modern callers he was been influenced by the false principles and distorted perspectives of the astray Muslim Brotherhood organization and its ideological leaders.

He failed to properly acknowledge that many scholars, and different similar knowledge based efforts, in various lands all across the world, are put forth by people proceeding upon the principles Sunnah to support, defend, and call to the true religion of Allaah. Sheikh Rabee'a Ibn Haadee, may Allaah preserve him, mentioning both living and deceased scholars stated,[5]

> *"Is there in the entire world one who is similar to Sheikh Ibn Baaz, and Sheikh al-'Utheimeen, and Sheikh 'Abdul-'Azeez Salmaan, and Sheikh Fauzaan, and Sheikh Hamoud at-Tuwayjaree, and Sheikh al-Ghudyaan, and Sheikh 'Abdur-Razzaq Afeefee, and Sheikh 'Aal -Sheikh?? Or similar to the many scholars of this land, as well as its students of knowledge?!*
>
> *Are there any similar to them in their character, sound beliefs, and struggles in the path of Allaah?! If only the various groups and parties brought forth or produced those who could be judged or regarded as similar to them.*
>
> *If only they brought forth the likes of Sheikh al-Albaanee, and his students; certainly they are those who are knowledgeable of the Sunnah and striving in the path or cause of Allaah's right to worshiped alone, combating all forms of associating others in Allaah's worship as well any forms of innovation in the religion.*
>
> *Or like the scholars of Hind, such as Sheikh 'UbaydAllaah al-Mubarakfooree, and his brothers in Islaam in Hind and Pakistan, in their practice of the religion, their good character, sound beliefs, efforts to make the truth known, and their patience with the suffering endured in the path of Allaah.*

---

[5] "The People of Hadeeth are the Victorious and Saved Group: A Knowledge Based Dialog with Salmaan al-'Awdaah":

Or bring forth an example similar to Sheikh 'Abdul-Baaree and his brothers in Islaam in Bangladesh! Offer to us an example similar to these individuals in their practice of the religion and excellence of character!

So how can it be that you could accuse the people upon this methodology of the first generations with a partisanship which segments the religion into different parts, and with avoidance of dealing with the affairs of Muslims, as well as a heedlessness and a turning their backs on the current state of the Ummah? Especially when they have among them the sheikh, the guiding scholar, the one who strives with high vigilance and watchfulness, and who closely follows the various states and conditions of the Muslims in every area of the world to such a degree that you would believe that if there was some beneficial efforts of Muslims was found on the planet "Mars", that he must be the one behind initiating it, and by this I refer to Sheikh Ibn Baaz!

Have you forgotten, oh Salmaan, the various conferences which have been established by those who follow this path and call in the various different areas of the world in order to educate the teachers in the various Muslims schools of the Ummah?

Have you forgotten the many educational scholarships established for study in the different Salafee educational institutions given to the sons of the Muslims coming from the entire world? Especially the Islamic University, which has designated that eighty percent of its students are those given scholarships from students of the various other countries of the Islamic world?! Have you forgotten the different centers established for calling to Allaah of which perhaps a hundred have been placed in the various places in the world?..."

All of this is stated based upon the unchanging principle of our religion has been affirmed and as stated generally by the leading scholars of every age including the above mentioned leading scholars. Indeed, centuries ago Sheikh al-Islaam Ibn Taymeeyah, may Allaah have mercy upon him said,[6]

> *"Truth in this religion is not connected to any specific person such that it revolves around him and never separates from him wherever he stand or goes, except for the Messenger of Allaah, may Allaah's praise and salutations be upon him.*
>
> *Since there is no one who is infallible and protected from falling mistakenly affirming something from falsehood other than him, may the praise and salutations of Allaah be upon him. As only he, the Prophet, is the established proof upon Allaah's creation, whom it is obligated that we follow him and obey him in every matter above any other person."*

Likewise, in our age, Sheikh Sulaymaan Ibn 'Abdullah Abaa al-Khayl, may Allaah preserve him, stated, [7]

> *"Every individual who attaches the truth to a specific individual, is someone them slipping into a dangerous abyss, and opposing the Sharee'ah of Allaah, His religion, what He has commanded, as well as what His Messenger commanded. Since every person has their statements taken from and can also be rejected, except the Prophet Muhammad. This is something which all the four well-known leading scholars of jurisprudence stood in agreement upon."*

---

[6] at-Tisa'eneeyah vol.2 pg. 904 – This is an important work in the refutation of the errors of Ash'arees and how they differ from the beliefs of the Companions and first generations of Muslims

[7] From the lecture Beneficial Counsel & Advices- Shawwaal 22nd, 1439

THE NAKHLAH EDUCATIONAL SERIES:

MISSION

The Purpose of the 'Nakhlah Educational Series' is to contribute to the present knowledge based efforts which enable Muslim individuals, families, and communities to understand and learn Islaam and then to develop within and truly live Islaam. Our commitment and goal is to contribute beneficial publications and works that:

Firstly, reflect the priority, message and methodology of all the prophets and messengers sent to humanity, meaning that single revealed message which embodies the very purpose of life, and of human creation. As Allaah the Most High has said,

❧ *We sent a Messenger to every nation ordering them that they should worship Allaah alone, obey Him and make their worship purely for Him, and that they should avoid everything worshipped besides Allaah. So from them there were those whom Allaah guided to His religion, and there were those who were unbelievers for whom misguidance was ordained. So travel through the land and see the destruction that befell those who denied the Messengers and disbelieved.* ❧ –(Surah an-Nahl: 36)

Two Essential Foundations

Secondly, building upon the above foundation, our commitment is to contributing publications and works which reflect the inherited message and methodology of the acknowledged scholars of the many various branches of Sharee'ah knowledge who stood upon the straight path of preserved guidance in every century and time since the time of our Messenger, may Allaah's praise and salutations be upon him. These people of knowledge, who are the inheritors of the Final Messenger, have always adhered closely to the two revealed sources of guidance: the Book of Allaah and the Sunnah of the Messenger of Allaah- may Allaah's praise and salutations be upon him, upon the united consensus, standing with the body of guided Muslims in every century - preserving and transmitting the true religion generation after generation. Indeed the Messenger of Allaah, may Allaah's praise and salutations be upon him, informed us that, *{ A group of people amongst my Ummah will remain obedient to Allaah's orders. They will not be harmed by those who leave them nor by those who oppose them, until Allaah's command for the Last Day comes upon them while they remain on the right path. }* (Authentically narrated in Saheeh al-Bukhaaree).

The guiding scholar Sheikh Zayd al-Madkhalee, may Allaah protect him, stated in his writing, 'The Well Established Principles of the Way of the First Generations of Muslims: It's Enduring & Excellent Distinct Characteristics' that,

"From among these principles and characteristics is that the methodology of tasfeeyah -or clarification, and tarbeeyah -or education and cultivation- is clearly affirmed and established as a true way coming from the first three generations of Islaam, and is something well known to the people of true merit from among them, as is concluded by considering all the related evidence.

What is intended by tasfeeyah, when referring to it generally, is clarifying that which is the truth from that which is falsehood, what is goodness from that which is harmful and corrupt, and when referring to its specific meanings it is distinguishing the noble Sunnah of the Prophet and the people of the Sunnah from those innovated matters brought into the religion and the people who are supporters of such innovations.

As for what is intended by tarbeeyah, it is calling all of the creation to take on the manners and embrace the excellent character invited to by that guidance revealed to them by their Lord through His worshiper and Messenger Muhammad, may Allaah's praise and salutations be upon him; so that they might have good character, manners, and behavior. As without this they cannot have a good life, nor can they put right their present condition or their final destination. And we seek refuge in Allaah from the evil of not being able to achieve that rectification."

Thus the methodology of the people of standing upon the Prophet's Sunnah, and proceeding upon the 'way of the believers' in every century is reflected in a focus and concern with these two essential matters: tasfeeyah or clarification of what is original, revealed message from the Lord of all the worlds, and tarbeeyah or education and raising of ourselves, our families, and our communities, and our lands upon what has been distinguished to be that true message and path.

METHODOLOGY:

The Roles of the Scholars & General Muslims In Raising the New Generation

The priority and focus of the 'Nakhlah Educational Series' is reflected within in the following statements of Sheikh al-Albaanee, may Allaah have mercy upon him:

"As for the other obligation, then I intend by this the education of the young generation upon Islaam purified from all of those impurities we have mentioned, giving them a correct Islamic education from their very earliest years, without any influence of a foreign, disbelieving education."

(Silsilat al-Hadeeth ad-Da'eefah, Introduction page 2.)

"...And since the Messenger of Allaah, may Allaah's praise and salutations be upon him, has indicated that the only cure to remove this state of humiliation that we find ourselves entrenched within, is truly returning back to the religion. Then it is clearly obligatory upon us - through the people of knowledge- to correctly and properly understand the religion in a way that conforms to the sources of the Book of Allaah and the Sunnah, and that we educate and raise a new virtuous, righteous generation upon this."

(Clarification and Cultivation and the Need of the Muslims for Them)

It is essential in discussing our perspective upon this obligation of raising the new generation of Muslims, that we highlight and bring attention to a required pillar of these efforts as indicated by Sheikh al-Albaanee, may Allaah have mercy upon him, and others- in the golden words, *"through the people of knowledge"*. Since something we commonly experience today is that many people have various incorrect understandings of the role that the scholars should have in the life of a Muslim, failing to understand the way in which they fulfill their position as the inheritors of the Messenger of Allaah, may Allaah's praise and salutations be upon him, and stand as those who preserve and enable us to practice the guidance of Islaam.

Similarly the guiding scholar Sheikh 'Abdul-'Azeez Ibn Baaz, may Allaah have mercy upon him, also emphasized this same overall responsibility:

"...It is also upon a Muslim that he struggles diligently in that which will place his worldly affairs in a good state, just as he must also strive in the correcting of his religious affairs and the affairs of his own family. As the people of his household have a significant right over him that he strive diligently in rectifying their affair and guiding them towards goodness, due to the statement of Allaah, the Most Exalted, ❦ **Oh you who believe! Save yourselves and your families Hellfire whose fuel is men and stones** ❦ *-(Surah at-Tahreem: 6)*

So it is upon you to strive to correct the affairs of the members of your family. This includes your wife, your children- both male and female- and such as your own brothers. This concerns all of the people in your family, meaning you should strive to teach them the religion, guiding and directing them, and warning them from those matters Allaah has prohibited for us. Because you are the one who is responsible for them as shown in the statement of the Prophet, may Allaah's praise and salutations be upon him, { **Every one of you is a guardian,** *and responsible for what is in his custody. The ruler is a guardian of his subjects and responsible for them; a husband is a guardian of his family and is responsible for it; a lady is a guardian of her husband's house and is responsible for it, and a servant is a guardian of his master's property and is responsible for it....}* Then the Messenger of Allaah, may Allaah's praise and salutations be upon him, continued to say, *{...so all of you are guardians and are responsible for those under your authority.} (Authentically narrated in Saheeh al-Bukhaaree & Muslim)*

It is upon us to strive diligently in correcting the affairs of the members of our families, from the aspect of purifying their sincerity of intention for Allaah's sake alone in all of their deeds, and ensuring that they truthfully believe in and follow the Messenger of Allaah, may Allaah's praise and salutations be upon him, their fulfilling the prayer and the other obligations which Allaah the Most Exalted has commanded for us, as well as from the direction of distancing them from everything which Allaah has prohibited.

It is upon every single man and women to give advice to their families about the fulfillment of what is obligatory upon them. Certainly, it is upon the woman as well as upon the man to perform this. In this way our homes become corrected and rectified in regard to the most important and essential matters. Allaah said to His Prophet, may Allaah's praise and salutations be upon him, ❖ **And enjoin the ritual prayers on your family...** ❖ *(Surah Taha: 132) Similarly, Allaah the Most Exalted said to His prophet Ismaa'aeel,* ❖ **And mention in the Book, Ismaa'aeel. Verily, he was true to what he promised, and he was a Messenger, and a Prophet. And he used to enjoin on his family and his people the ritual prayers and the obligatory charity, and his Lord was pleased with him.** ❖
-(Surah Maryam: 54-55)

As such, it is only proper that we model ourselves after the prophets and the best of people, and be concerned with the state of the members of our households. Do not be neglectful of them, oh worshipper of Allaah! Regardless of whether it is concerning your wife, your mother, father, grandfather, grandmother, your brothers, or your children; it is upon you to strive diligently in correcting their state and condition..."

(Collection of Various Rulings and Statements- Sheikh 'Abdul-'Azeez Ibn 'Abdullah Ibn Baaz, Vol. 6, page 47)

Content & Structure:

We hope to contribute works which enable every striving Muslim who acknowledges the proper position of the scholars, to fulfill the recognized duty and obligation which lays upon each one of us to bring the light of Islaam into our own lives as individuals as well as into our homes and among our families. Towards this goal we are committed to developing educational publications and comprehensive educational curriculums -through cooperation with and based upon the works of the scholars of Islaam and the students of knowledge. Works which, with the assistance of Allaah, the Most High, we can utilize to educate and instruct ourselves, our families and our communities upon Islaam in both principle and practice. The publications and works of the Nakhlah Educational Series are divided into the following categories:

Basic: Ages 4- 6
Elementary: Ages 6-11
Secondary: Ages 11-14
High School: Ages 14- Young Adult
General: Young Adult –Adult
Supplementary: All Ages

Publications and works within these stated levels will, with the permission of Allaah, encompass different beneficial areas and subjects, and will be offered in every permissible form of media and medium. As certainly, as the guiding scholar Sheikh Saaleh Fauzaan al-Fauzaan, may Allaah preserve him, has stated,

"Beneficial knowledge is itself divided into two categories. Firstly is that knowledge which is tremendous in its benefit, as it benefits in this world and continues to benefit in the Hereafter. This is religious Sharee'ah knowledge. And secondly, that which is limited and restricted to matters related to the life of this world, such as learning the processes of manufacturing various goods. This is a category of knowledge related specifically to worldly affairs.

…As for the learning of worldly knowledge, such as knowledge of manufacturing, then it is legislated upon us collectively to learn whatever the Muslims have a need for. Yet If they do not have a need for this knowledge, then learning it is a neutral matter upon the condition that it does not compete with or displace any areas of Sharee'ah knowledge…"

("Explanations of the Mistakes of Some Writers", Pages 10-12)

We ask Allaah, the most High to bless us with success in contributing to the many efforts of our Muslim brothers and sisters committed to raising themselves as individuals and the next generation of our children upon that Islaam which Allaah has perfected and chosen for us, and which He has enabled the guided Muslims to proceed upon in each and every century. We ask him to forgive us, and forgive the Muslim men and the Muslim women, and to guide all the believers to everything He loves and is pleased with. The success is from Allaah, The Most High The Most Exalted, alone and all praise is due to Him.

Abu Sukhailah Khalil Ibn-Abelahyi
Taalib al-Ilm Educational Resources

TAALIB AL-ILM | BOOK PREVIEW

30 Days of Guidance [Book 1]: Learning Fundamental Principles of Islaam

A Short Journey Within the Work Al-Ibaanah al-Sughrah With
Sheikh 'Abdul-'Azeez Ibn 'Abdullah ar-Raajhee

AUTHOR - COMPILER - TRANSLATOR

Abu Sukhailah Khalil Ibn-Abelahyi

BOOK OVERVIEW

- Interactive course book
- Focused upon both beliefs & principles
- 1st book in 30 Day Series

WHO IS THIS BOOK FOR

All age levels

For every Muslim who wishes to live their life in a way pleasing to Allaah it is essential that they ensure that their beliefs and practices actually have evidence and support from within the sources of Islaam. This work approaches this challenge in a way that allows an individual to proceed through discussions related to this a day at a time over thirty days, based upon explanations from one of today's noble scholars.

WHAT YOU WILL LEARN IN THIS BOOK

Related to essential basic principles of guidance

The role of Islaam in today's world is something which is indisputable and often contested. There are many different understandings of Islaam which range from dangerous extremism, all the way to vulnerable laxity. Yet our well-known scholars continue to work diligently in openly examining and clarifying the false ideas and practices that are attributed to Islaam.

PRICING

- *Hardcover -USD $45.00*
- *Soft cover -USD $27.50*
- *Kindle -USD $09.99*

PDF PREVIEW

https://ilm4.us/30daybook1

PURCHASE BOOK

http://taalib.com/4134

TAALIB AL-ILM | BOOK PREVIEW

30 Days of Guidance [Book 2]: Cultivating The Character & Behavior of Islaam

A Short Journey Within The Work Al-Adab Al-Mufrad With Sheikh Zayd Ibn Muhammad Ibn Haadee al-Madkhalee

AUTHOR - COMPILER - TRANSLATOR

Abu Sukhailah Khalil Ibn-Abelahyi

BOOK OVERVIEW

- Interactive course book
- Focused upon both character & behavior
- 2nd book in 30 Day Series

WHO IS THIS BOOK FOR

All age levels

This course book is intended for the Muslim individual for self-study, as well as for us as Muslim parents in our essential efforts to educate our children within Islaam and our ongoing endeavor of cultivating them upon the extraordinary character and behavior of our beloved Prophet. It is also intended to be an easy to use classroom resource for our Muslim teachers in the every growing numbers of Islamic centers...

WHAT YOU WILL LEARN IN THIS BOOK

Related to the subject of perfecting ones character

Some of the questions that this course book helps us answer are: Are you prepared for your reckoning? Are you always working for good while you can? Do you remember the benefit in your difficulties? Is your life balanced as was the lives of the Companions? How do you deal with your own faults and those of others? Do you know what things bring you closer to Jannah?....and more

PRICING

- *Hardcover - USD $45.00*
- *Soft cover - USD $27.50*
- *Kindle - USD $09.99*

PDF PREVIEW

https://ilm4.us/30daybook2

PURCHASE BOOK

http://taalib.com/4137

TAALIB AL-ILM | BOOK PREVIEW

Foundations For The New Muslim & Newly Striving Muslim

A Short Journey through Selected Questions & Answers with
Sheikh 'Abdul-'Azeez Ibn 'Abdullah Ibn Baaz

AUTHOR - COMPILER - TRANSLATOR

Abu Sukhailah Khalil Ibn-Abelahyi

BOOK OVERVIEW

- Interactive course book
- Focused upon essential beliefs & challenges
- 4th book in 30 Day Series

WHO IS THIS BOOK FOR

All age levels

This course book is intended for both the person who has newly embraced Islaam or that Muslim or Muslimah whom Allaah has blessed to now have the resolve within themselves to truly turn towards their Most Merciful Lord and commit themselves to becoming a better worshipper upon knowledge. It for that individual who, regardless of the direction they came from, wishes to change both the inward and outward aspects of their lives to now move in a direction truly pleasing to Allaah.

WHAT YOU WILL LEARN IN THIS BOOK

Related to building a firm foundation for our Islaam

This course book discusses What are the conditions of correct Islaam? Is faith only what is in our hearts? When is it necessary for me to ask a scholar? What is the guidance of Islaam about our health? What should I do after falling into sin again and again? Do I have to make up for my previous negligence? How should I interact with the non-Muslims I know? and more...

PRICING

- *Hardcover -USD $45.00*
- *Soft cover -USD $27.50*
- *Kindle -USD $09.99*

PDF PREVIEW

https://ilm4.us/30daybook4

PURCHASE BOOK

http://taalib.com/4147

TAALIB AL-ILM | BOOK PREVIEW

30 Days of Guidance [Book 3]: Signposts Towards Rectification & Repentance

A Short Journey through Selected Questions & Answers with
Sheikh Muhammad Ibn Saaleh al-'Utheimeen

AUTHOR - COMPILER - TRANSLATOR

Abu Sukhailah Khalil Ibn-Abelahyi

BOOK OVERVIEW

- Interactive course book
- Focused upon both change & growth in Islaam
- 3rd book in 30 Day Series

WHO IS THIS BOOK FOR

All age levels

This course book is intended for any Muslim who wishes to improve his life and rectify his heart. Yet this self rectification or purification of the soul must be done in the correct way and upon the correct foundation of knowledge from the Sunnah, if it is to lead to true success in both this life and the next. Ibn al-Qayyim, may Allaah have mercy upon him, also stated, 'The true purification of the soul and the self is directly connected to those messengers sent to humanity..."

WHAT YOU WILL LEARN IN THIS BOOK

Related to the Subject of perfecting ones character

This course discusses in detail the inward and outward changes and steps we must take as striving Muslims to improve and bring our lives into a better state after mistakes, sins, slips, and negligence. Discussing real life problems and issues faced by Muslim of all ages and situations -the Sheikh advises and indicates the road to reform, repentance, and true rectification.

PRICING

- *Hardcover -USD $45.00*
- *Soft cover -USD $27.50*
- *Kindle -USD $09.99*

PDF PREVIEW

https://ilm4.us/30daybook3

PURCHASE BOOK

http://taalib.com/4150

TAALIB AL-ILM | BOOK PREVIEW

Statements of the Guiding Scholars of Our Age Regarding Books & their Advice to the Beginner Seeker of Knowledge

[Contains A List of over 300 Books Recommended By The Scholars In The Various Sciences Of Islaam]

AUTHOR - COMPILER - TRANSLATOR

Abu Sukhailah Khalil Ibn-Abelahyi

BOOK OVERVIEW

- Taken from words of senior scholars
- Provides road map for Sharee'ah study
- Divided into seven main sections

WHO IS THIS BOOK FOR

All age levels

A comprehensive guidebook for the Muslim who wishes to learn about his or her religion with the proper goal and aim, in the proper way, and through the proper books. This question and answer book is for those who seek advice from some of the senior scholars of the current century regarding seeking knowledge, against books containing misguidance.

WHAT YOU WILL LEARN IN THIS BOOK

Sources and subjects of seeking Sharee'ah knowledge

This book is intended to enable any sincere Muslim to strive to proceed with correct methods and manners in seeking of beneficial knowledge for themselves and in order to guide their families. The scholars are the carriers of authentic knowledge and the inheritors of the Messenger of Allaah. Their explantations make clear for us the way to learn and then live Islaam.

PRICING	PDF PREVIEW	PURCHASE BOOK
• *Hardcover -USD $45.00* • *Soft cover -USD $27.50* • *Kindle -USD $09.99*	 https://ilm4.us/seeker	 http://taalib.com/79

TAALIB AL-ILM | BOOK PREVIEW

An Educational Course Based Upon Beneficial Answers to Questions On Innovated Methodologies
of Sheikh Saaleh Ibn Fauzaan al-Fauzaan

AUTHOR - COMPILER - TRANSLATOR

Abu Sukhailah Khalil Ibn-Abelahyi

BOOK OVERVIEW

- Interactive course book
- Focuses upon principles of the straight path
- Discusses modern groups and movements

WHO IS THIS BOOK FOR

All age levels

This course book is for any Muslim who wishes to understand the detailed guiding principles of Islaam as discussed by the scholars throughout the centuries, including the scholars of our age. These principles were initially put in place and practiced by the generation of the Companions of the Messenger of Allaah, may Allaah be pleased with all of them, when Islaam was first established, and have been implemented in each and every century by those Muslims following in their noble footsteps.

WHAT YOU WILL LEARN IN THIS BOOK

Related to the detailed way we understand Islaam

This course focuses upon the importance of clarity in the way you understand and practice Islaam. What is the right way or methodology to do so? Examine the evidences and proofs from the sources texts of the Qur'aan and Sunnah and the statements of many scholars explaining them, that connect you directly to the Islaam of the Messenger of Allaah.

PRICING

- *Hardcover -USD $50*
- *Soft cover -USD $32.50*
- *Kindle -USD $09.99*

PDF PREVIEW

http://ilm4.us/minhaj

PURCHASE BOOK

http://taalib.com/4144

TAALIB AL-ILM | BOOK PREVIEW

The Belief of Every Muslim & The Methodology of The Saved Sect

Lessons & Benefits From the Two Excellent Works of Sheikh Muhammad Ibn Jameel Zaynoo

WHAT YOU WILL LEARN IN THIS BOOK

Related to foundation of Islaam & gaining knowledge

This Islamic studies course discusses the different levels of knowledge, important matters related to seeking knowledge, essential study skills, the role of evidence in Islaam, differing and taking from the scholars. Additionally, it explains the central role that the foundation that worshipping Allaah alone should have in our lives, and how that distinguishes every single person.

AUTHOR - COMPILER - TRANSLATOR

Abu Sukhailah Khalil Ibn-Abelahyi

BOOK OVERVIEW

- Interactive course book with diagrams
- Discusses how to study and from whom
- Focuses upon both beliefs & practices

WHO IS THIS BOOK FOR

All age levels

This course book is for any Muslim who is looking for an easy-to-follow course- based discussion of not only what it is important to learn but also concise advice on how to study and learn Islaam. Taking selections from two well-known books of Sheikh Zaynoo, may Allaah have mercy upon him, it offers an overview of some of the characteristics and hallmarks which distinguished that clear call our beloved Prophet brought to humanity.

PRICING	PDF PREVIEW	PURCHASE BOOK

- *Hardcover -USD $45.00*
- *Soft cover -USD $30*
- *Kindle -USD $09.99*

https://ilm4.us/savedsect

http://taalib.com/4141

TAALIB AL-ILM | BOOK PREVIEW

The Cure, The Explanation, The Clear Affair, & The Brilliantly Distinct Signpost

Book 1: Sources of Islaam & The Way of the Companions- *A Course Upon Commentaries of Usul as-Sunnah' of Imaam Ahmad*

AUTHOR - COMPILER - TRANSLATOR

Abu Sukhailah Khalil Ibn-Abelahyi

BOOK OVERVIEW

- Interactive course book with 15 lessons
- Focuses upon sources & principles of Islaam
- First book in continuing series

WHO IS THIS BOOK FOR

All age levels

This course book is intended for any Muslim who wishes to connect himself to our beloved Prophet. inwardly and outwardly, in order to walk in his footsteps upon knowledge as a worshiper of Allaah. It is designed to help you, as a Muslim, identify the correct sources, principles, and beliefs of the evidenced methodology of Islaam upon scholarship and proofs, in order to be able to distinguished what opposes them from incorrect sources, principles, and false beliefs.

WHAT YOU WILL LEARN IN THIS BOOK

Related to the independent sources of Sharee'ah guidance
This course book discusses the universal nature and correct beliefs about Islaam as a revealed religion. It also discusses specifically what are the correct evidenced beliefs held by the people of adherence to the Sunnah throughout the centuries about the nature of the Qur'aan, the Sunnah and scholarly Consensus.

PRICING

- *Hardcover -USD $45.00*
- *Soft cover -USD $30*
- *Kindle -USD $09.99*

PDF PREVIEW

https://ilm4.us/usulbook1

PURCHASE BOOK

http://taalib.com/62874

www.ingramcontent.com/pod-product-compliance
Lightning Source LLC
Chambersburg PA
CBHW022116040426
42450CB00006B/720